MY
TEENAGER
IS DRIVING
ME CRAZY

MY TEENAGER IS DRIVING ME CRAZY

A GUIDE TO GETTING YOU
AND YOUR TEEN THROUGH
THESE DIFFICULT YEARS

BY JOYCE L. VEDRAL, PH.D.

ADAMS MEDIA CORPORATION
Avon, Massachusetts

Published by
Adams Media Corporation
57 Littlefield Street, Avon MA 02322. U.S.A.
www.adamsmedia.com

ISBN: 1-58062-919-9

Printed in Canada.

J I H G F E D C B A

Library of Congress Cataloging-in-Publication Data
Vedral, Joyce L.
My teenager is driving me crazy / Joyce L. Vedral.
Updated and rev. ed.
p.   cm.
ISBN 1-58062-919-9
1. Parent and teenager. I. Title.
HQ799.15.V43 2003
306.874--dc21
2003004476

This publication is designed to provide accurate and authoritative information
with regard to the subject matter covered. It is sold with the understanding that the
publisher is not engaged in rendering legal, accounting, or other professional
advice. If legal advice or other expert assistance is required, the services of a com-
petent professional person should be sought.
  —From a *Declaration of Principles* jointly adopted by a Committee of the American
      Bar Association and a Committee of Publishers and Associations

Many of the designations used by manufacturers and sellers to distinguish their
products are claimed as trademarks. Where those designations appear in this book
and Adams Media was aware of a trademark claim, the designations have been
printed with initial capital letters.

This book is available at quantity discounts for bulk purchases.
For information, call 1-800-872-5627.

Table of
Contents

Dedication

This book is dedicated to my mother, Martha Yellin, who never gave up on me, her most difficult teenager—the one who almost drove her crazy. If it were not for her frequent reiteration of some basic truths about life and her relentless belief that her words would someday take root (I gave her no indication that she was getting through to me), I would not be the person I am today. I would not have written this book. I would not have achieved my goals in life. And what's more, I wouldn't have the most precious gift she gave me by her example: a simple faith in a very loving and uncomplicated God.

And to my father, the late David Yellin, for believing in me and letting me know it, and for teaching me that life is an obstacle course—and that I had the power to jump the hurdles.

To both of you, I apologize for giving you the hardest time—but I thank you for never giving up on me. It was your loving persistence that saved this life.

■ ■ ■

Acknowledgments

To the thousands of teenagers and parents I've interviewed—from all over the United States and many from other countries as well.

—To Kate McBride for having a vision for this book.

—To Courtney Nolan.

—To my daughter Marthe and her many teenage friends who taught me the true meaning of being a parent.

—To my family and friends, for your continual support and help.

—To my parents: see the dedication!! I love you, I love you, I love you.

■

Introduction

What do I mean by a teenager? A teenager is a born-again three-year-old trying on his or her wings. Don't try to tell a teenager how to fly, because, like the three-year-old, a teen has a very strong will. But you would never stop trying to tell your three-year-old what to do, would you? Obviously, it would result in disaster. The same holds true for a teen, except the way you tell a teen what to do is quite different. You guide your teen. You use psychology. You keep in mind that your teenager has a "full deck" in the intelligence department, but he or she is not yet worldly wise. It's your job to clue your teenager in without alienating him or her.

There's much more in store for parents today than simply worrying about alienating their teens. First, the teen years start even before a child reaches the age of 13! Years ago, a teenager was a child, literally, between the ages of 13 and 19, but that's not true today! Children are growing up faster than most parents like, so when we talk about teens we're talking about children as young as 10 years old! Also, there are more dangers today. Drugs, sexually transmitted diseases, violence, and bullying are just some of the things that parents have to be careful to warn their teens about. I could go on and on. But wait! With guidance from you—as long as you don't quit on the job (and I know you won't or you wouldn't be reading this book)—your teen can walk over the minefields and make it through just fine.

As you continue reading, you will gain insight into exactly how your teen is thinking, and you'll find ways to show your teen how *you* are thinking. You'll get through to your teen in ways you never dreamed. You'll be delighted to find that you're not alone—this will comfort you—and you'll get some ideas on how to handle situations without making them more explosive. You'll find ways to calm things down and keep your sanity.

No matter how "crazy" it gets, no matter how out of control you feel, keep in mind that "this too shall pass." If you're anything like me, before you do anything important regarding your teen, you'll take out an insurance policy by shooting up a simple prayer to God. "Give me wisdom, God. You know everything. What would you do in this situation?" Whenever I remembered to pray that prayer, I did not make a mistake. And you don't have to be religious to reach out to God for help. Think of it this way: If there is a God, wouldn't he want to support you and give you and your teen the best possible chance for a happy life?

A final word—this time about me. I've spent 20 years teaching teenagers in the high school environment, and in this sense you can call me a spy. I have a gift with teens. They tell me things they would never tell their parents. This is how I can give you an insight into how they think, and some advice on how to get through to them. You'll find out the surprising reasoning behind why they say what they say and do what they do. You can read the chapters in this book in any order—as needed in the moment of crisis—but please read the entire book. And remember, no matter how crazy it gets, believe it or not, someday you'll look back at these days with a smile and, yes, of course, with a sigh of relief!

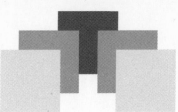

Chapter 1
My Teenager
Is Driving Me Crazy

Most teenagers put their parents to the test on a daily basis. They are often demanding, unappreciative, irresponsible, or defiant. They frequently criticize their parents, hang out with the wrong crowd, dress outrageously, flaunt annoying habits, refuse to communicate, and are inconsiderate of others. At times, they seem to be doing all these things with a calculated plan. (But of course, no plan is needed. Their actions are quite natural.)

My teenager is driving me crazy. She thinks I'm a bank—there's no end to her demands—yet when I ask her to do a simple chore, I have to remind her so many times that she accuses me of being a nag. If she's not wearing her hair teased up in points like the Statue of Liberty, she's hanging out with girls who make hookers look conservative. When I try to talk to her about sex, school, her future, or any other serious matter, all I get is "Yeah, I know, I know, Mom." She blasts her stereo, stays on the phone for hours, lies about everything, and makes me wonder if she's doing drugs, because one minute she's as happy as a lark and the next minute she looks as if she's thinking about committing suicide. I tell myself, "It's normal teenage behavior. Why don't I lighten up? I'll take a long, hot shower and forget my woes.

I reach up to the shelf for my shampoo and it's gone. "I'll kill her," I think as I grab a towel and run, dripping, up the stairs to retrieve my shampoo from the upstairs bathroom." I finally get my hair shampooed, only to look in the mirror and see that those locks are graying rapidly. I don't wonder why.

Your teenager may not be on drugs (at least you hope not). She isn't pregnant (and you even have hopes that she's not sleeping around). He isn't failing every subject in school. She may not be threatening to run away from home. So far, he's had no trouble with the law. But nevertheless, from one day to the next, your teenager is driving you crazy.

You ponder, "What in the world makes that boy tick? *How does his mind work?*" You ask yourself, "Am I getting through to her, or are all of my lectures going in one ear and out the other?" You ask, "How can I make him open up to me—get him to confide in me?" You wonder, "Is it possible to get her to have some compassion toward me to see my side of it for a change?"

What You Can Expect from This Book

1. You will find out how your teenager's mind works, and gain insight into the strange things he or she does, such as why she expects you to buy her designer clothing even though she knows your income is limited, and why she tells you how to dress, wear your hair, and behave in public; why he won't talk to you about sex; why she lies to you and sneaks behind your back to see that forbidden boy; why he refuses to do a simple chore, even though he's been reminded a thousand times; why she comes home late even though she knows an ugly scene will follow; and why you're usually the last to know when

something potentially tragic is going on in your teen's life. You'll find out how to change all these things.

2. You will discover where your nagging and lectures are being lodged in your teenager's mind. You'll learn what effect your words have upon him when he is about to do the wrong thing and may discover, perhaps to your surprise, that many of your lectures and much of your nagging have already been quite effective. You will learn that if you stopped lecturing, your teenager's behavior will worsen. *You'll learn more effective ways to insure that your teen is absorbing your values.*

3. You'll learn how to tailor pep talks to your teenager's mind, for maximum effect when a moment of decision arrives and you are not at the scene.

4. You'll discover what your teenager *really* worries about during the course of a typical day, and find out how to be of comfort so that the worry doesn't deepen into depression.

5. You'll discover how to get your teenager to confide in you when something is on his mind, but your self-control will be heavily tested in the process. (You'll have to wait until the next day to deliver any homilies.)

6. You'll find out that your teenager does have compassion for you; it's just that she rarely expresses it. You'll learn how to get your teen not only to show compassion, but to increase it. You'll end up with a teenager who is less self-centered and more appreciative of what you do for her, and who appreciates *your* own good qualities.

7. You'll feel generally more comfortable about being the parent of a teenager in this changing world.

Every Parent's Dream

Whether we admit it or not, we all get a secret thrill when we find evidence that our teenager is taking on our values. You may have already had an experience similar to that of these parents.

■ "I couldn't believe my ears. One day I overheard my daughter talking on the telephone. She was discussing the behavior of one of the girls in her crowd. I heard her say: 'If Andrea keeps smoking pot, she's going to end up a real loser. You know, it's been proven that people who smoke pot lose their motivation. It destroys brain cells. What a waste.' You can imagine how thrilled I was. Before that conversation I wasn't sure if my continual speeches about the harmful effects of drugs were getting through her thick skull. Until that moment, for all I knew, she could have been smoking marijuana in the school bathroom every day." 45-YEAR-OLD MOTHER

■ "My son really surprised me. He came home from school one day and said, 'Dad, John makes me sick. He came over and told me how proud he was that he got 100 on the social studies test. Then he started bragging about how well his cheating system had worked. I could have vomited. I mean, if I cheated, and got a high mark, I wouldn't be bragging about it, I would secretly know that I was a fraud, and that the mark was a lie. It's one thing to cheat. That's bad enough, but to be proud of yourself for it, I mean, this guy thinks he can get through life by cheating. You know what I told him? I said I'd rather get a 75 and know the mark was mine than 100 and know it had nothing to do with what I could really do. He called me a jerk and walked away. He's the jerk. Not me.' After that conversation I thought it looks like I've been getting through to him after all. Amazing." 43-YEAR-OLD FATHER

What is our primary goal as parents? To instill in our offspring values that we believe will get them through life in the best possible way. What are your values? What is it that you wish your son or daughter would learn now and use as a guideline through life? By way of example, I'll list some of my values here.

My Philosophy

1. Every person has something to contribute to the world; you were born for a reason. Find out what your purposes are and determine to fulfill your potential. The ultimate goal is to discover your gifts and use your potential to the fullest extent.

2. Hard work and steady effort are most likely to result in eventual success. Instead of turning frustration against yourself when you fail at something, you can sublimate the anger and use it as energy to overcome the next obstacle.

3. Worry is unproductive. It's much better to simply hold your concern up to God in the form of a prayer asking him to work things out for the best, as he knows all things. Then sleep on it, and the next day begin your active search for an answer. This will bring a serene mindset that will aid the emergence of the answer you need.

4. The mind is the most powerful tool you have. It will

ultimately make you a success or a failure. We all need every bit of the intelligence we have, and cannot afford to sacrifice one IQ point by doing drugs.

5. The mind is the most advanced computer available. You can use your subconscious mind to help you solve problems, by posing a question and waiting, alert, for it to deliver the answer.

6. The things we do, good or bad, eventually come back upon us. As if planting a crop, if you work hard, treat others the way you wish to be treated, and are generally kind, loving, compassionate, and generous, sooner or later a whole field of love, compassion, and success will grow up in your life. If, on the other hand, you continually cheat and are cruel or hardhearted, you will attract bad luck. You will subconsciously draw it to yourself.

7. Put a high value on your family. Friends may come and go, but chances are your family will always be there for you.

8. Be loyal. Keep your word.

9. Avoid lies. They tangle you up. Honesty is liberating.

10. Maintain your independence and boundaries. Never completely surrender yourself to anyone. Don't think you can't live without someone no matter who it may be. That person is a gift to you. If he or she is taken away, remember, you still have yourself. As long as you're alive, wonderful things can happen in the future. Life is a great adventure.

What Are Your Values?

Although you've already been teaching your teenager your values by way of example, it's helpful to zero in on exactly what those values are. Make a list of them. It's the only writing I'll ask you to do in this book. But this is very important, so please do it.

In attempting to list your values, at first you may say, I don't know where to begin. You can be as concrete or as philosophical as your nature allows. For example, you might list such things as:

- Get a good education.
- Treat people with fairness.
- Be loyal to your friends.
- Save money for the future.

After you make your list, decide which values are the most important, and put a star next to each one. You'll probably notice that those ideas are the theme songs of most of your lectures to your teen.

Never Too Late

Now is the perfect time to start making changes. Your teenager's mind is receptive and will internalize what you present to him or her. Past mistakes will be quickly forgotten as you begin making the right moves with your teenager. I've seen miracles happen. They can happen for you and your teen as well.

Chapter 2

What Have You Done for Me Lately?

One of the most frustrating things about being a parent is not the giving, but the feeling that most of the time it's being taken for granted. Most parents do not have an endless supply of money, and no parent has endless energy, yet we are continually being asked to give and give and give of both.

■ "Money doesn't grow on trees; you don't just go out with a sack and pick some. Wait until you earn your own money then talk." 41-YEAR-OLD MOTHER

■ "Do you think I go out from nine to five and just sit around all day?" 47-YEAR-OLD FATHER

■ "I'm tired of being everybody's slave!" 38-YEAR-OLD MOTHER

Since money is the biggest bone of contention in most families, we'll discuss it first.

Give Me, Give Me, Give Me

Parents constantly complain that their teenagers want them to buy things that are either unaffordable, ridiculously overpriced, unnecessarily luxurious, or just not appropriate. What is the strange logic of the teenage mind? What do teens expect their parents to buy for them and why?

■ "Makeup. Where else am I going to get the money? I'm too young to get a job, besides babysitting." KATY, 13

■ "Hazel contact lenses. I need glasses or contacts anyway, so for a few dollars more they could get me the color lenses instead." MARY, 15

■ "My father said when I get married, I'll have to marry a millionaire when I asked for $100 sneakers. He doesn't understand, the new styles cost that much." DONNA, 16

■ "More clothes. When I say I have nothing to wear, my father says, look in your closet. It's full of clothes. But those styles are out now. All I hear from him is, I want things, too. But I can't get them because I've got bills to pay." DEBBIE, 16

■ "A pair of Gucci shoes for $265, because I want them so I can be a happier person." JOAN, 15

■ "A gold bracelet with my name in diamonds. I got a good report card." MISHA, 17

■ "A car, because all my friends have one. I don't want to be riding public transportation." MIRIAM, 17

■ "A $3,000 notebook computer. Parents say they want you to learn a lot, but then they don't provide you with the equipment you need. They want you to learn the hard way." NATASHA, 17

■ "Drums. It may be worth it in the future. I might be a professional drummer." SAMMY, 17

Let's look at how these teens think. Katy reasons, "I can't get the money myself, so they should give it to me." But she isn't dealing with the fact that her parents disapprove of their 13-year-old daughter wearing makeup in the first place. Katy's parents should be more direct: "We don't approve of girls your age wearing more than a little lipstick, but if you want to spend your hard-earned babysitting money on makeup, that's your business." They can also add a speech about how makeup actually detracts from her looks, and how they can't wait until she's an older teen, when she will see that for herself. (Teens do learn such lessons; see Chapter 7.) Katy will get the message. "My parents cannot be expected to finance me in things they disapprove of. I'll have to either find a way to pay for them myself now, or wait until I can."

Mary does not perceive that her parents' reason for not getting her the contact lenses has nothing to do with practicality. They don't approve of her changing her eye color. In fact, when I asked Mary's mother about the lenses, she said, "I am totally against it, because I feel she has to be satisfied with the eyes she was born with. The eyes are the windows of the soul. If you change your eye color, you hide your real self."

Most teenagers can detect excuses, and they resent hearing them because they perceive excuses as insincerity. It's always best to level with a teenager. Instead of telling teens they can't afford something (when they *can* afford it), or making other false excuses, parents should put their cards on the table. For example, if Mary's mother expressed what she told me to Mary, and added: "When you get a job, you can spend *your* money on color contact lenses if you wish," Mary would probably resolve to get regular contacts herself.

Donna, Debbie, Joan, and Misha need to be made aware of the family budget. Their parents should sit them down one day and say something like: "I'm figuring out my monthly bills. Could you help me for a minute?" I did this with my daughter.

I called out the amount of each bill, and she wrote it down. Then I asked her to get a total for me. When she did that, I asked her to subtract the total from my monthly income. There was $300 left. "Uh-oh," I said. "This month the car insurance is coming up. That's $150. Looks like I'll have to wait until next month to get the new rug for your room."

"Oh, that's okay," she said. "Another month won't matter." And then with a sheepish grin, she added, "I was going to ask you for money for boots, but if you don't have the money, it's all right." And by the look on her face I could tell she was thinking some new thoughts.

She had begun to get the picture, and your teen will, too. There's no need to get into a screaming match. If you invite your teen in on your real-life situation and treat him or her as a comrade instead of an enemy, your teen will, in fact, become an ally.

But even if parents *do* have an abundant supply of money, teens need to be made aware that things just won't come to them endlessly. Miriam believes that she is owed a car just because all of her friends have cars. Not so. She should be encouraged to save for a car and perhaps go half with her parents on a used car when enough money is accumulated. That's the deal I made with my daughter when she was a teen, and she valued the car more.

Natasha and Sammy believe that since they're eager to become successful in the future, and are willing to put in the effort, they should be subsidized by their parents. To a point, of course, they're correct. Parents *should* subsidize their teens, but only in order to *help them to help themselves*—and they must be made to see the difference between a necessity and a luxury.

A $3,000 laptop computer is not a necessity. Less expensive ones can be bought new at half the price, and a used one would be even less. Sammy can buy used drums or save up enough to buy them himself.

Teenagers are learning, and parents are the ones who are doing most of the teaching, whether the parties involved are aware of it or not, every day. If, for example, Sammy's parents wave him off and say, "You don't need drums; it's a waste of money—you'll never be a professional drummer," they are teaching him that it's a waste of time to pursue his inner voice, his musicality and, perhaps, his creative ability and they will be hindering his effort to find his identity. If Miriam's parents allow themselves to be conned into getting her a car, she will be in for a rude awakening up the road, when she finds out that her parents will not always be with her to help.

You Take Everything for Granted

Parents complain that their teenagers are unappreciative.

■ "You are never satisfied. If you had holes in your shoes, you would be happier." 49-YEAR-OLD FATHER

■ "You take everything for granted. I'm tired and my feet hurt. Once in a while you can do something for me." 41-YEAR-OLD MOTHER

Sound familiar? But what many parents don't realize is, teenagers often feel grateful for what their parents do for them, but neglect to express that appreciation.

■ "I thank her in my own way by wearing what she bought me." MARSHA, 15

■ "Sometimes I forget to thank her because I'm so used to her generosity, but I'm really thankful that she's not cheap with me." MARTHE, 16

■ "Sometimes I'm embarrassed to make a big deal of it." LISA, 14

■ "I feel they know I love them and appreciate anything they do." TRINA, 15

■ "Sometimes it slips my mind, but I do appreciate it." FRAN, 13

Silent appreciation. What a shame. Here is a group of teenagers who sincerely appreciate what their parents do for them, but their parents would find it hard to guess that. Small wonder parents often feel resentful, even furious, when going the extra mile is routinely ignored.

If your teen neglects to acknowledge your special efforts to make his or her life easier, you'll have to be the one to make the first move. The next time your teen's failure to respond leaves you feeling high and dry, say something like: "I really went out of my way to [fill in the blank], and I couldn't wait to see your reaction. I was very disappointed when you acted as if it meant nothing to you. Did you appreciate it?" If you don't get a satisfactory answer, get more specific. You might say "I was tired and didn't feel like going from store to store to find that exact jacket you've been talking about all month. But I kept thinking of how much you wanted it, and I forced myself to go. In the store, I was thinking, I can't wait to see his face when I give it to him. Now all I get is a grunt." Express disappointment, rather than anger, in your tone of voice. Nine out of 10 times, a teen will respond to such an appeal. He'll probably say something like "Oh, I'm sorry, Mom. I do appreciate it; it's just that I have a lot on my mind."

"But I don't want to have to ask him to thank me," you say. Put aside false pride. Communication is the goal here. Clear the air whenever there is lack of communication *before* misunderstanding and resentment have a chance to build.

Another way to help teens become more aware of how precious your time is, how you have daily chores to complete, and to help teens learn responsibility would be to ask your teen to help out, perhaps by preparing dinner once a month. This responsibility would not only help the teen understand how much work is involved in doing something "simple" like preparing a meal, but it would be fun for the teen, and build his self-esteem because you've entrusted him with such an important duty.

The teen would be given a budget for the dinner and then have to shop for the ingredients. Then he would have to create a menu plan—either a simple one that does not require a cookbook, or a more elaborate meal (depending on his age and experience level). A parent could supply a couple of recipe books to help.

The teen would come home from school, go food shopping (a parent might have to help with a ride to the supermarket), and then prepare the meal. The wake-up call would be: "Gee, I can't sit and watch TV or get on the phone. I have to use my time wisely. Mom does this all the time. I guess her life is not so easy." And the teen would think differently the next time he made an unrealistic demand around dinnertime!

One of the best ways to teach your teen to show appreciation is to remember to show it when your teen does something special for you. Often, many of us merely think about how wonderful it was that our teen did such and such; we neglect to mention it because he or she is not around at the moment we're thinking about it, or we're not in the mood to make a big deal out of it at the time the good deed is done. For example, one day, my daughter did an extra special job in cleaning the house. She did far more than her usual share of the work because I was sick. But I had a fever and was drifting in and out of sleep, so I just thought about how thoughtful she had been; I didn't tell her. Two days later I remembered and said: "Marthe, you did such a good job cleaning the house for me when I was sick, and I didn't even thank you. You have no idea how much I appreciated it. I should have thanked you two days ago. I feel bad." She beamed and said, "It's all right, Mommy." I could see she was delighted to have the recognition, even though it was late.

We've heard it a million times. Children learn more by one example than by 100 sermons. My philosophy is, keep them both going—the examples *and* the sermons. Children learn from sermons, too! Even if they say they don't. (See Chapter 10.)

The Most Generous Thing My Parents Ever Did

Not only do teenagers appreciate many of the things their parents do for them, they will remember certain things for life, specific acts that will come to symbolize the basic goodness of your relationship. However, it's usually years later that parents find out—if ever. Luckily for me, I found out how much something I had done for my daughter meant to her. Just to see what she would say, I asked her to fill out the question sheets I asked other teens to complete in preparation for my writing this book. To one of the questions, "What is the most generous thing your parents ever did for you?" she wrote, "When you took me and Jennifer to the Bahamas, I thought you were the best mother in the world."

I don't remember her making a big deal of thanking me during the trip or once we had returned home. Although I thought it seemed we all had a good time, I do recall asking myself, when it was over, if I had really made very good use of a lot of time, money, and energy. My goal had been to get some sunshine and to create permanent positive memories for my daughter, but I had no idea I had succeeded until, months later, I read her response.

My daughter is far from unusual in this area. Hundreds of teenagers appreciate what parents do for them, though for one reason or another, they may neglect to tell their parents so. Here's some proof. I asked teens "What is the most generous thing your parents ever did for you?" Every teen I asked had something to say.

▪ "They took me to Victor's Cafe for my birthday. I felt so special, so sophisticated. I'll never forget it." JANET, 17

▪ "When I was 11, they took me to Bermuda. I didn't want to leave my friends that Christmas vacation, but I had the best time. I still think about it." NICK, 15

■ "When I was 14, they let me go to Action Park with my older sister, when I had begged all day to go. I was so happy I wanted to cry." NINA, 18

■ "My mother took me down south when I was 13. I saw my grandmother, my aunts, and my cousins. They were really cool. Now we write each other all the time, and I'm going back next year." SANDRA, 16

■ "They gave me a bank account starting with $500. I was shocked. After that I started saving money in bits and pieces. Now I've got a real stash." RONNY, 17

■ "My mother gave me her credit card and let me shop with it by myself for my birthday. I felt like a rich lady." ANGELA, 16

■ "My mother stayed home because I asked her to. I wanted her to keep me company watching this movie on TV. I felt so happy." ROCHELLE, 15

The things you do for your teen on special occasions, during vacations, and (often spontaneously) from day to day are part of the family ties you create in your teen's mind. They will bind you lovingly together forever. Parents' generosity does not escape the notice of their children. In fact, it helps to shape children's personalities.

By the way, don't let their protests stop you. It's not unusual to have to pry teens away from their friends, persuade them to leave the sofa where they're watching television, and practically break their arms to get them to go somewhere with you. You'll most likely find out that they had the time of their lives, as did Nick, whose parents insisted on taking him to Bermuda.

Even the small things count. I remember with nostalgia my reluctant trips with my father to the local ice cream parlor when I was 12. I didn't want to go; I even remember hoping that I wouldn't run into any of my friends on the way. But as I recall, I actually felt sorry for my father. I knew he was trying to get close to me, and that made me feel loved. At that age, my understanding was unconscious, rather than conscious. What was then a mixed blessing is now a sweet memory.

Think of your own life. What precious memories do you have of your mother or father doing special things with and for you?

I Really Do Appreciate Your Help

Parents continually go out of their way to do things for their teenagers that seem to be routinely taken for granted. They:

- Drive her to school early in the morning, instead of sleeping that extra hour.
- Take him back and forth to soccer practice, instead of making him walk home.
- Help her with her homework, do her laundry, and straighten up her room if she's busy.
- Fill out college applications, buy him new clothes, take him to get his car fixed.

Do teens take these things for granted, or are they aware that you went out of your way? I asked teenagers the question "What have your parents done for you lately?" Here's what they said.

■ "My mother drove me to my friend's house when I had no way to get there." DENISE, 16

■ "My father picked up my clothes from the cleaners." DANNY, 17

■ "My mother came to school and got me out of hot water with the principal so I didn't get suspended." JOEY, 16

■ "My mother knew it was my turn to wash the dishes last night, but when I fell asleep doing my homework, she did them for me." JACKIE, 16

Were these teens aware that their parents had gone the extra mile? And if so, did they let their parents know? Of course not. In fact, I believe the teens themselves may not have been consciously aware until asked the question "What have your parents done for you lately?"

Most teens would feel bad if they knew that their parents had to make big sacrifices for them just so that their children's lives could be a little easier. When asked how they would feel if they knew their parents were considering making such a sacrifice, they say:

■ "I would feel bad, and let them do what they want to do. It's probably more important." ERROL, 16

■ "I wouldn't want it that badly anymore." JARED, 18

■ "I feel sad because my parents worked hard their whole lives for me. Now it's time for me to give up something for them." SIMONE, 16

■ "I would feel selfish because they give up a lot for me as it is." EMILY, 15

Most teenagers are compassionate. They do have tender hearts but they're not about to give away their feelings easily. How can you find out how your teenager feels about the many things you do for him or her? One way is to have your teen fill out the questions in the appendix at the back of this book. Parents reported that when they read their teen's answers to the questions, they were amazed to discover how their teens really felt.

How Much Should You Do for Your Teens?

It's impossible to leave this topic without at least mentioning a problem that most parents struggle with. How much should I do for my teen? Am I spoiling him and turning him into a Mama's boy? Or, on the other hand, am I doing too little and focusing too much on my career at the expense of my children?

I remember having to grapple with that question when my daughter was invited to a prom. As it turned out, her date had made up his mind to wear a deep purple cummerbund and it was my daughter's job to obtain a prom gown to match. When we talked about going shopping for the dress, a big argument ensued, because Marthe expected me to take her shopping as many times as it took to find the dress. In the meantime, I have a more-than-full-time job as a teacher, writer, lecturer, and so on.

As we sat in the orthodontist's office, arguing about the dress, I could hardly suppress tears of frustration. Filled with all sorts of mixed emotions, I realized I was feeling both guilty and angry. Analyzing my emotions, I figured out that I was feeling guilty because I expected myself to be 100 percent at my daughter's service, and angry because my life did not allow that. Very selfishly, I wished that I had someone to pamper me for a change and actually resented the fact that I didn't have someone to do that for me. I then realized how ridiculous my guilt was. I was making impossible demands on myself. I waited until we got in the car, and instead of continuing to vent my spleen, I explained to my daughter exactly how I was feeling.

I told her how frustrated I was because I have so much to do, and couldn't spare as many days for shopping as some of her friends' mothers could. I then said: "I can set aside two shopping days for your dress. After that, you'll have to go on your own." To my surprise, Marthe brightened up and agreed that was fair enough. In a better mood, we went shopping and, as luck would have it, found *the* dress that very day. But the best luck for me was not in finding the dress. It was realizing that, as parents, we are the ones who have to set the limits of how many extra miles we will go, and that most teenagers respond reasonably once we've helped them to become aware of our real-life imperatives.

Reminders

1. If your teenager believes she deserves certain luxuries just because they will make her happy, sit her down and ask her to help you add up the monthly bills and figure out how to pay them.
2. If you don't want to buy something for your teenager because you disapprove of it, say so.

3. Remember to express your appreciation for things your teenager does for you. Your personal example is crucial.

4. Do special things with your teenager. You'll be helping him build permanent lifetime memories, which will become more and more special as time passes. In spite of his initial protests, he will appreciate your caring, whether or not he tells you so.

5. If you're not getting the appreciation you think you should get, ask for it. Express your feelings exactly. "I was really excited about [fill in the blank] and was disappointed when you didn't say a word." Again, you are modeling direct communication for your teen by doing this.

6. Use the question sheets in the appendix at the back of this book to find out more about how your teenager feels.

7. Give yourself a break. Instead of feeling guilty about not going the extra mile, have a talk with your teenager and work out a fair arrangement.

Chapter 3

Wake Up
and
Smell the Coffee

This chapter will not only help you to understand why teens neglect to fulfill even the most basic responsibilities and commitments, but it will also show you how to motivate them to change that behavior. It will also help you to understand why teenagers waste time and why they often resist engaging in what parents feel are productive activities.

- "Her room is a sty. Will she *ever* clean it? I ask myself, What did I do wrong?" 35-YEAR-OLD MOTHER
- "An hour late and no call. I don't know whether to think the worst, or say: 'There he goes again.'" 43-YEAR-OLD FATHER
- "I worry that she won't even finish high school. It's murder to get her to study." 39-YEAR-OLD MOTHER
- "What's wrong with you? You knew about that appointment three weeks ago!" 42-YEAR-OLD FATHER

Why are teenagers irresponsible? Is it procrastination or just sheer laziness? Are they living in a dream world?

Clean Your Room, Take Out the Garbage, Pick Up the Towels

You're not a slave driver. You don't ask for much—only that he do his part as a member of the family. Why do teenagers neglect even the most simple chores? Teens say:

■ "The living room looked fine to me. I said to myself, Why do I have to straighten it up now? It will be here when I wake up tomorrow." MARSHA, 15

■ "The vacuuming never got done because I got an important phone call and when I got off, I forgot." ALLISON, 16

■ "The bathroom is very hard to clean. I felt tired when I thought of doing it." KATY, 13

■ "I didn't feel like washing the clothes so I said, 'Watch my mom do it later.' And she did." BARBARA, 17

■ "I did not have time to sweep the stairs because she wants everything done in one day. I sweep, mop, wash dishes, and do the laundry. Then I have to do my homework and get my clothes ready for school the next day. Sometimes I think I'm going crazy. I lied and said I swept them and they got dusty again." LESLIE, 15

■ "If I cleaned my room, I wouldn't be able to find what I'm looking for." RICK, 16

■ "I'm always mowing the lawn, and then they have the nerve to say I never do anything. What do these people think I am, their slave?" MIKE, 16

Notice that each teen has given some thought to the neglected chore. First, Marsha rationalizes: The living room doesn't really need straightening up. But apparently Marsha's reasoning fails to convince even her so she procrastinates. Of course, the job never gets done. One way to help teens not to procrastinate is to take casual advantage of available opportunities to be a good example. For example, you can say "I'm filing my income tax now, in February. This way it's off my back. You never know what will come up next month, and I don't like to make unnecessary pressure for myself."

Allison became distracted by the phone call, then forgot to vacuum the house. Most parents don't believe teens when they say, "I forgot," but very often that excuse is the truth. Teens need to be helped to remind themselves to fulfill their responsibilities. A list pasted on the wall where things can be crossed out after they're done works well.

Parents continually say to teens: "You're young; you have more energy than I do." While that's true, teens do get tired and sometimes when, like Katy, they are faced with an arduous chore, they picture all the work involved and feel defeated before they start. If I were Katy's mother, I would tell her "I know how you feel before you start a task. You can feel exhausted and wonder how you will ever get the energy to complete it. But once you force yourself to get up and get started, after a few minutes you'll have more energy, and the time will fly and the job will get done. After the first five minutes, you'll wonder why you felt so tired in the first place. All you really needed was to start your motor, and when you finish the chore, you'll feel happy that you accomplished it—and the best part is, then you'll be free to enjoy doing something else. What's more, the next time you're faced with a task that looks like a biggie, you'll remember your recent, successful experience, and that will help you get *that* job done, too."

Barbara's mother is teaching her to be irresponsible by doing Barbara's undone chores herself. Barbara will quickly pick up on a new reality when her mother lets the dirty clothes pile up until, finally, Barbara is forced to wash them because she has run out of things to wear.

However, at times you will find that solution unfeasible: Maybe you just can't stand the sight of even a few dirty dishes in the sink, much less teetering stacks of them sprouting mildew. In such a case, it's wise to consider the price of the battle and perhaps give up on trying to get your teen to do that particular chore.

This is what happened with my daughter and me. She would willingly do all of her other chores, but when it was her turn to do the dishes, she would procrastinate all night, and I would end up nagging and getting upset. So I finally decided that I would do all the dishes from then on. But she would have to pay the price: She would not have her own telephone line. We discussed it, and she agreed. She would rather share my telephone than do the dishes. But I was happy, too, because our deal meant I would not have to pay an additional phone bill. If she wasn't willing to do her part, why should I hand over the extras, the luxuries?

The beauty of our resolution? Neither party to the bargain would harbor resentment against the other; neither had lost a battle. At the same time, both my daughter and I were spared the daily stress of fighting over dishes that take 10 minutes to do.

Sometimes teens refuse to do chores because they are being unfairly overloaded with tasks. Leslie's demanding schedule has forced her into a corner. She figures the only way out is to lie. Obviously, her parents are overloading her with household chores and it's not fair to her. If your teen complains that her day is too full, sit down and have her write out a daily schedule from wake-up time to bedtime. Either you and your teen will find a place to schedule in the chore or you will realize that the schedule is too tight and will cut back on the demands.

Rick evidently likes his room a mess. It's *his* mess, and he claims he won't be able to find anything if he straightens it up. His parents can let him keep his room the way he wants as long as he keeps his door closed to avoid offending the general run of humanity passing by, and as long as he doesn't leave food around that will attract bugs. After all, it *is* his room, the only room in the house that is his own private property. Or another deal can be struck. Once a week, and on special request when company comes, the room gets cleaned and straightened out by Rick.

Many teens don't so much mind doing chores but do mind a lack of recognition for what they do. What would it cost Mike's father to say something like: "Mike, when I come home from work tired, and see that lawn mowed, it puts me in a good mood for the evening. You have no idea what a help that is to me."

Another way to get your teen to be more responsible about chores is to provide him or her with something to look forward to—a vacation from chores. After all, even adults look forward to vacations. Teens do get a vacation from school, but when do they get a vacation from chores? You can provide that vacation, and even let your teen pick his or her vacation time.

Do Your Homework, Study for the Test, Work on the Report

Parents wonder how their teens will ever graduate from high school—forget about making it into a good college.

■ "I never see you study. Don't you have any homework? When are you going to do the research for that report?"

■ "I didn't get where I got in life by looking around and hoping to get lucky. I worked hard. When are you going to wake up?"

Why don't teens fulfill their school responsibilities? We'll start with the least responsible teens and work our way to the most conscientious. When asked why they neglect their schoolwork, teens say:

▧ "It's boring. I just say, the hell with it." DANIELLA, 15

▧ "I figure I'll just give an excuse. Maybe they'll let me slide." LISA, 15

▧ "Oh well, it's only schoolwork. I'll just have to kiss up to the teacher when it's report card time." DANNIK, 17

▧ "If I miss a deadline, I'll just be absent." ALEXIS, 15

▧ "I figure I can make it up and hand it in late." ARTHUR, 17

▧ "When I wait until the last minute, it's because I just can't get myself to get it done. I say, I'll do a rush job and get a lower grade." MARY, 15

▧ "I knew I was going to get a bad grade, but at the time I was arguing with my boyfriend, so it didn't matter to me. I was too upset." DENISE, 16

▓ "I'm a senior, and I just don't care. The more I think about it [the college average has already been computed], the more I say, big deal." JARED, 18

▓ "I am usually very responsible. If I don't get it done, it's because of my busy schedule and because I had to put the more immediate things first." THEO, 18

The first four teens are irresponsible, because they evidently don't see the importance of doing the work. What they need is a goal.

My own daughter was getting low grades during her freshman year of high school until we sat down and had a talk about what she wanted to be in life. She had known for a few years that she wanted to be a psychologist, but we never really got into the details of what it would take to achieve that goal. Once we discussed how she would have to be accepted into a good college and possibly continue going to school after she received her bachelor's degree, she began to make a connection between her dream for the future and her grades now. In what seemed like an overnight transition, she became a responsible student working persistently at studies that (she claimed) bored her, such as memorizing facts about medieval history and managing to do well in her difficult math class. When she saw the tangible result of an increased overall average of 14 points for the first marking period (we had our talk in the summer), I said, "I'm impressed. You decided to put in more effort, and I see the result in black and white." She beamed and said, "If I don't keep my grades up, I'll never get into a good college." Marthe received Phi Beta Kappa and magna cum laude honors when she graduated from college. Yet I remember how hopeless I was feeling the day I had that chat with Marthe. This little voice kept saying, "You're wasting your time," but I started on my "To get into a good college, you have to work hard" talk. Parents, KEEP TALKING NO MATTER WHAT!!

If a teenager has a goal—one that the teen believes good grades in school will help him or her to achieve—a teen is less likely to avoid schoolwork by making excuses, kissing up to the teacher, being absent on due dates, and procrastinating.

Mary, Denise, Jared, and Theo are not really irresponsible. They are actively engaged in the battle that adults fight all of their lives: how to take care of business despite inertia, emotional upsets, and limited time.

If I were their parents, I would be pleased that they are well on their way to becoming responsible adults. Such teenagers need a listening ear much more than a sermon on responsibility.

You're Late!

Most teenagers are at least reasonably alert. Why, then, parents wonder, can't they do so simple a thing as to arrive home on time, or at least call? But often, certain logic underlies their actions or their inaction.

■ "I know when I'm late I won't get in much trouble, so if I'm having a good time, what's the problem?" RICHIE, 16

▪ "When I don't come home on time, I just think of what excuse to give them." LOUIE, 15

▪ "I picture them yelling at me until I start crying and going into my room, slamming the door. Why do I do it anyway? I just can't leave yet. We're having too much fun." PAULA, 14

▪ "My mother says it worries her to death when I don't call if I'm late, but if I'm having a great time, I'm usually too lazy to get to a phone. I know it's wrong, but that's just what happens." SIMONE, 16

▪ "I only live once. Why be an angel twenty-four hours a day?" TONY, 15

Richie and Louie know they won't really get in trouble if they're late, so why should they come home on time? Think about it: What are the actual consequences if your teen comes home late time and again? You may not have analyzed your actions until now, but is it possible that your teenager is not punished appropriately when he or she is late?

Many teens know there will be a scene if they're late, but they're willing to pay the price because it isn't high enough to affect their actions. Paula pictures the unhappy scenario ahead of time, but figures it's a reasonable price to pay for the pleasure of staying out late. Her parents probably have a screaming match with her and leave it at that. Rather, I would save my energy and subtract the late time from her next night out. If she's late that time, too, I would ground her. Now, Paula is good at visualization. She would picture herself coming home early next time or having to sit at home the next Saturday night. Such visions may well change her behavior.

Simone's mother is dramatic about how she feels when Simone is late but not specific about how important it is for her daughter to obey the rules. Teenagers really do respond to concerned and worried parents, but they need to have a clear picture painted. One teen read this mother's account and had an interesting if not surprising reaction:

■ "My daughter said she would be leaving her friend's house at 11:00 and would be home at about 11:15. The girl lives five blocks away, but it's not the best neighborhood. She promised that if her plans changed and she left the girl's house earlier, she would call. At 11:30 she still wasn't home, so I called her friend's house to find out that she had left at 10. I hung up the phone and felt my whole body tighten up. I pictured her walking home and someone grabbing her into a car. I called her other girlfriend, hoping she stopped there. When the girl said she hadn't heard from her, I could hardly control my voice. Tears were coming. I said thank you, and hung up. I jumped in the car and drove around for 10 minutes. When I got home, I thought, surely she'd be there. I called her name, but no one answered. I started to pray. 'Oh, God. Please help me. If only she's all right.' I was just about to call one of her other friends and ask her to come cruise the neighborhood with me for all possible places she might walk. Just then the door opened. Now it was after midnight. She was smiling and happy. I started screaming, 'Where were you?' She said, 'Oh, I forgot to call. I went over to Rob's house.'" 34-YEAR-OLD MOTHER

The teen said:

▧ "My God. I never really thought about it before—how we make them suffer when they don't know where we are or why we're late. I'm going to call my mom next time I'm late." JOHANNA, 16

If your teenager is insensitive to your worry, sit her down and take her through your typical thought process as the clock ticks away in her absence. Chances are, the next time she feels tempted to be insensitive to your worry, she'll imagine your mental agony and make an effort to be considerate.

Tony's reason for lateness points up a simple truth about many teenagers: They get tired of playing it straight and want to rebel once in a while. It sounds to me as if Tony is usually reliable. If I were his parents, I would reinforce his positive behavior by saying something like: "Tony, you're usually very responsible, so we're not going to punish you this time, but if it happens again, and you don't call, there will be consequences."

Is Anybody in There?

They forget to give you important messages, lose their keys, lend out their expensive clothing and then buy replacements in the wrong size, get up late for school, neglect their pets, and drop their clothing everywhere.

What in the world is going through their minds? you wonder. When asked why they're irresponsible in specific areas, teens have said the following.

■ "Someone had called for my mother, but after I took the message, I went back to watching TV. Then I just forgot." BILLY, 15

■ "I know I should always keep my keys in one place, but I'm absentminded. I daydream a lot, and I can't remember what I did with them." SUNNETTA, 16

■ "I like to wear my friends' clothes, so I have to let them wear mine." MARTHE, 16

■ "They want me to buy things that will fit next year, too, but I like tight clothing so I get a small size, even though I know they'll yell." MISSY, 17

■ "When the alarm goes off, I'm too lazy to get out of bed even though I know I'll be late for school." BRIDGETT, 14

■ "My mom drops her clothes wherever she wants when she's tired, so I just think like mother, like daughter." SANDRA, 15

Teens have very specific reasons for their lack of responsibility, and if we listen to their reasons, we can help them.

A pad and pencil next to each telephone would take care of Billy's problem. His responsibility would end once he wrote the message down. To reinforce the new drill, his parents could write his messages down on the pad, too. I got special "while you were out" message pads, and my daughter and I worked out a deal: I leave her messages on the stairs leading up to her room, and she leaves mine on the kitchen table. Every once in a while she forgets to write down an important message. When that happens, I tell her exactly what inconvenience her lapse caused, and she apologizes. If it happens too often, I might consider forgetting a message or two I had taken for her to drive home the point.

Sunnetta has evidently been lectured about misplacing her keys. If I were her mother, I would ask Sunnetta, "Should we get a neck chain? Or maybe you could keep your single key in the change purse of your wallet. What about a key case, to be kept in the zipper compartment of your book bag?" Then I would buy her (or give her money to buy) a new item that would solve the problem of misplacing keys.

The next time I went shopping with Marthe, and she wanted me to buy her expensive clothing, I would say, "I would love to buy this for you, but I picture Stacey wearing it, and that makes me angry since I'm not working to dress Stacy in style. If we could make a deal . . ." Then we'd make a deal, any violation of which (after an initial grace period) would mandate that no new clothing (except for vital items) be bought the next shopping time.

Missy's problem could be solved by refusing to let her go shopping alone. I would give her one more chance to show good judgment, but after that I would say: "Since I can't afford to buy you clothing that doesn't fit, I'll have to insist that I go with you either until your judgment improves or you're earning your own money."

Getting out of bed is a whole different problem. Most people wouldn't mind getting an extra hour's sleep in the morning, but responsibilities force them to get up, so they think of the fresh coffee they will get to drink, or the new outfit they have laid out to wear, or the happy lunch date they have, and then they drag themselves out of bed. Bridgett could be helped by this method. For some, it can be as simple as the thought of a refreshing hot shower or the fact that spring vacation begins next week.

The next issue involves role modeling. Sandra notices that her mother throws her own clothing on the floor, so she excuses herself for doing the same. A good example is worth one thousand lectures, but parents do have special privileges. (Whether it's wise or fair to invoke those privileges habitually is another matter entirely.) If her mother cannot or will not set an example, she still has the right to say: "I am the one paying the bills, and I'm responsible for keeping the house clean so I can mess up the house as I will, but you can't. If I see your clothing on the floor, I'm going to throw it on your bed."

Do Something Productive

It drives parents up the wall to see teens whiling their hours away wasting time. Parents shout:

■ "Your face didn't change any since the last time you looked in the mirror."

■ "Why don't you take your bed into the street? You're never home anyway!"

■ "Stop watching those stupid wrestling matches."

■ "I'm canceling your cell phone."

■ "Dance lessons, what a joke. You should be studying algebra instead."

What productive activities do parents think their teenagers should engage in, and what do teens think about those activities?

Go to the Library

▨ "When I'm hanging out with my friends, my mother says, 'Why don't you go to the library?' I need time with my friends. What, does she expect me to be a hermit?" DAISY, 14

Message: "Be realistic, Mom. I need a social life, too."

Work on Your Vocabulary

▨ "My mother gets annoyed when the first thing I do in the morning is put on the TV. She says, 'Why don't you listen to vocabulary tapes instead of wasting your time?' She's right about it being better to accomplish things than watch TV, but when I first wake up on the weekend, I want to relax, not run around getting things done." VALENTINA, 16

Message: "You may be a workaholic, but I'm not.
Give me a break."

Get a Job

▨ "My mother says I play too much hockey. 'Why don't you get a job?' That's all I hear. But what is stupid to her is important to me. I have to work the rest of my life. I want to have fun now." JARED, 18

Message: "I don't want to rush into adult life. It's obviously not as much fun as being a teenager."

Read the Bible

■ "I like listening to the radio because I enjoy hearing the latest songs. Music picks up my mood. But she says, 'Read a book, look at the news, read the Bible.'" RITA, 15

Message: "Those things make you happy. Music makes me happy. Get off my back."

Get Some Exercise

■ "I collect pictures of stars and hang them up in my room. My mother says 'Go out and play basketball, soccer, ride your bike, or something. Get some exercise.' But I hate sports, and I just want to enjoy my day the way I want to enjoy it." GARNET, 15

Message: "Let me pursue my own interests. I'm not harming anyone, am I?"

Participate in Extracurricular Activities

■ "I like writing songs and poems, but my mother says 'Why don't you join the extracurricular activities at school?' I'm planning to be a singer someday and write my own lyrics. I don't really like my school or the people in it and I don't want to spend my afternoons in that grim building when I can go home and relax and work on my music." JAIMIE, 16

Message: "See it from my perspective, then talk."

Get Some Sleep; You Look Like a Zombie

▨ "I take a long time getting dressed for school in the morning because if I don't look my best, I feel uncomfortable in school all day. My mother says, 'If you spent that extra hour getting your rest, you wouldn't look like a zombie in the morning.'" DANA, 15

Message: "I have my priorities. To me,
looking good is worth the price of losing a little sleep."

Spend More Time with the Family

▨ "I spend a lot of time at my boyfriend's house. My mother says, 'Why don't you spend more time with the family?' But sometimes, family activities are boring." ROSANNA, 17

Message: "I want to spend time with my boyfriend.
I'm a teenager. I don't want to be like the Brady Bunch."

Practice Your Clarinet

▨ "I read and collect comics. My parents say, 'Why don't you spend your time practicing your clarinet?' I'm losing interest in the clarinet. But now I got my grandfather interested in comics. He's a Vietnam veteran, so every time I buy comics he tells me to pick up *Nam Nam* [a comic book about real-life happenings in the Vietnam War]." JOSE, 15

Message: "I'm moving on to another stage. Let me.
If I can't fight you, I'm clever enough to get you to join me."

Do Volunteer Work

■ "When I talk to people on the psychic phone line, my mother says, 'Why don't you do volunteer tutoring instead of wasting time and money talking to phonies who don't really know you and are just making things up?' It's interesting to see what they say about your future, but tutoring to me is boring." FRAN, 17

Message: "I need more adventure in my life."

Join a Youth Group

■ "I love dancing and I go to a special school after class. My mother says 'Why don't you join the Jewish Youth Group?' But to me, those people are just a bunch of snobs. I'd rather be dancing than wasting my time with them." TARA, 16

Message: "I'm more sensitive than you realize.
Please allow me to follow my own lead."

Join the ROTC

▪ "They think everything I do is dumb. I like to iron my socks because they look nice. She says 'You're too fussy. Why don't you join the ROTC? That will get the primp out of you real fast.' But I hate that uniform." JACKIE, 16

> **Message:** "I have my own ways.
> Try to accept me instead of trying to change me."

As parents, we like to say "I don't understand." It seems to me, a more accurate statement would be "I understand, but I don't like what I understand."

So what's a parent to do? Should we give up on our ideals and just let our teens watch TV, talk on the telephone, spend hours in cyberspace, hang out with their friends, neglect their homework, and never accomplish anything? Of course not. We should continue to encourage them to participate in stimulating activities—while remaining realistic. Teenagers need their own time to do whatever they want, too. How they spend this time, is not a waste. If we continue to point out the value of certain activities, and to be an example of what we preach, most teenagers will (amazingly) turn into responsible adults . . . who still, once in a while, waste time. (Don't you?)

Reminders

1. Help your teenager not to procrastinate, advising him or her indirectly by relating specific ways you tackle tasks.

2. Help your teen to be more responsible by making a list of chores to be done, and pasting it up in your teen's room. Leave a pad by the phone for message taking.

3. Teens do have more energy than parents, but they often find themselves burdened by overloaded schedules and become physically and mentally tired. Help your teen to evaluate his or her schedule, and if it's overloaded with chores, eliminate some, or help him or her schedule activities.

4. Help your teen to fulfill responsibilities with the "once you get started and how great you feel after" method.

5. Sometimes a chore isn't worth the rancor that surrounds it. You are the parent; you can cancel a chore if you want to. It may be easier for you to do it yourself.

6. Teens need things to look forward to. Give your teen a vacation from chores.

7. To motivate your teen not to neglect schoolwork, find a way to link schoolwork with his or her hopes for the future.

8. To help your teen to be more considerate about lateness, paint a vivid picture of what goes through your mind when he or she is late.

9. Motivate your teen to get up in the morning by teaching him or her to invent a personal goal of what to look forward to, whether it be a lunch date that day, or the spring vacation that's coming next week.

10. When your teen engages in unproductive activities, keep on explaining what would better occupy his or her time, but realize that teens need some time to do what pleases them.

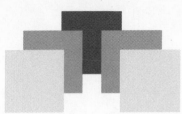

Chapter 4
I'm the Mother,
You're the Child

I n this chapter you'll discover that you're not the only parent
who is routinely corrected on how to dress and behave.

■ "I know, I know, that's all you hear. Isn't it amazing that
a 16-year-old can know it all?" 42-YEAR-OLD FATHER
■ "She actually tries to dress me. You're not going *with me*
dressed that way, she says." 37-YEAR-OLD MOTHER
■ "She thinks I'm out of it, a throwback from the sixties."
44-YEAR-OLD MOTHER
■ "He must have the last word, regardless." 39-YEAR-OLD
MOTHER

Teens tell us how to dress and wear our hair, and criticize
our behavior. They defy our rules because, they say, we don't
know what's happening. When their smug pronouncements
aren't completely frustrating or infuriating, they're really funny.
No wonder parents often find themselves shouting at their
teen: "I'm the mother, you're the child!"

In this chapter, you'll find out why teens often openly defy
their parents and, to your surprise, you may discover that such
behavior is not always done with the intention of disrespecting
you. You will also find out what lies behind the seemingly hard
exterior of a teen who is being rebuked, and you'll be happy to
know that your teenager often feels deep compassion and

concern for you as he or she takes on the temporary role of being a parent to you.

You're Not Wearing That, Are You, Ma?

Parents complain:

■ "I'm still young, why shouldn't I dress it? They don't appreciate a young mother." 35-YEAR-OLD MOTHER

■ "I may dress old-fashioned, but I don't have to impress anyone now." 41-YEAR-OLD MOTHER

■ "If we dress to be hip, they complain that we're trying to look like a teenager. If we don't dress according to fashion, they brand us old-fashioned. Why do teens make a big deal about the way we dress?" 34-YEAR-OLD MOTHER

In answer to their parents' complaints, teens say:

■ "My father wears these long slacks that go past his shoes. He looks like a geek." TYRONE, 16

■ "My mother was wearing these tight pants. I told her they didn't look correct. I don't want guys looking at my mother that way." MARQUITA, 16

■ "I couldn't believe my father was going to leave the house wearing those bike pants. He looked foolish." RITA, 14

■ "She wore something that was in the back of the closet from the seventies. I said, 'Where in the world are you going with that? Uh-uh, not with me. You're not my mother. I'm saying I adopted you.'" MARSHA, 15

▪ "My mother wears this green housedress with flowers on it, and it makes her look fatter than she already is. It bothers me because I don't like to see her looking sloppy and ugly." MYRA, 14

▪ "My father wears shirts that are too tight with big collars. I want my parents to be in style." KATY, 13

▪ "My mother looks stupid in this favorite skirt of hers." LAURETTA, 16

▪ "When my mother wants to wear one of my outfits that is very teenagelike, I tell her it doesn't look right. I don't want people to laugh at her. But she says, 'Oh, you just don't want me to look good.'" BRENDA, 16

▪ "My father wears these faded, washed-out jeans. I can't stand them. What does he think, that he looks sexy in them?" MIRIAM, 17

▪ "My mother has crow's feet and varicose veins and she wore this pink miniskirt. I told her to take it off because I didn't want her to be embarrassed." RUBY, 16

▪ "She wore these bell-bottom pants. I begged her not to wear them. I don't want her to look like she doesn't know what's going on." LINDA, 18

Loose pants, long pants, tight pants, bike pants, flowered dresses, seventies dresses, miniskirts, eighties hairstyles, teen outfits, big collars, faded jeans, bell-bottoms. Teens issue rebukes against such sins of parental apparel because they believe they're protecting us from making fools of ourselves. (And maybe they are, but some of us don't care. We're happy making fools of ourselves, and wish to be left alone.)

They don't want us to look *too* up-to-date, but on the other hand, they don't want us to look out of style. They don't want us to look sloppy and fat, but it's even worse if we look too sexy. In short, they want us to look motherly or fatherly. Neat and conservative. Not conspicuous. Teens want their parents to have class.

We don't know any better, so they must tell us. But if you read between the lines, they're doing more than saving us. They're saving themselves embarrassment. Just as we see our children as reflections of ourselves, teens see us as reflections of themselves.

But what's a parent to do? Should we change our basic dress style just to accommodate our teenagers? Not completely, but I think it's a good idea to be sensitive to their feelings. For example, I used to work out in a gym located in a shopping mall, and after working out, I'd do some shopping with my gym shorts on. My daughter, who was 13 then, would die of embarrassment. Somehow I understood her feelings, so I modified my habit because it seemed a small enough imposition. If my daughter was with me and I knew we were going to walk around the mall, I would bring something to change into.

Teens Criticize Their Mothers' Hair and Makeup

Mothers don't understand why their teens criticize their appearance so much.

■ "It makes me sad that she can't give me a compliment and make me feel good for a change. When she said, 'Your hair looks like wings,' I told her to get the hell out of my room and leave me alone." 43-YEAR-OLD MOTHER

Here's what some teenagers say about correcting their mothers' makeup and grooming.

▪ "That makeup made her look pale. I couldn't ignore it because she looked like a vampire." WENDY, 16

▪ "She tried to put curls in her hair and it looked really stupid, so I told her I couldn't have her look like a dummy in front of everybody." ROSIE, 15

▪ "I had to tell her about that red lipstick. She looked like a clown. If I didn't, somebody else would have." BRIDGETTE, 16

▪ "She wanted to shave the sides of her hair. I told her I would have a fit. I didn't want people talking about her." NICOLE, 17

Some things will never change. Children still can't stand anyone even thinking (much less talking) negatively about their mothers. They feel it is their obligation to defend us. And if they agree with the criticism others make at our expense, our teens become more angry with us for offending their personal tastes and for jeopardizing their fledgling social position. Self-preservation causes them to try to head us off at the pass, before we make fools of ourselves and them.

Embarrassing

As parents, we've really got to mind our p's and q's. It's not easy to avoid embarrassing your teenager, especially if you like to dance, make jokes, or let off some steam once in a while. Teenagers lament:

■ "My mother was dancing in the street. She looked stupid." JOSHUA, 14

■ "When I had my sweet sixteen party, my mother got in the middle of the floor and started darting around. She looked like she was having an epileptic fit, but I guess she thought she was dancing. I didn't like that too much." HEATHER, 17

■ "When my father tried to learn the new dances, I told him to give it up. If he went to a party and did that, they would probably kick him out." SAMANTHA, 15

■ "When my mother drinks rum she acts worse than a damn kid." KELLEY, 16

■ "My father thinks when we have company, he's a great entertainer, but he's just acting immature. I didn't tell him, but I wish he wouldn't be so childish and make a scene." JAIME, 16

■ "My father likes to make jokes, and he acts retarded. It's kind of funny, but it's embarrassing." AMY, 13

■ "My father was driving me and my friends to a party, and on the way over, he started to sing songs he knew, and tell stupid jokes about my room and about how it's such a mess, you need a map to find your way around. My friends found this to be funny, but I didn't." DENISE, 15

■ "When my mother talks to my bird in a baby voice, I feel embarrassed for her." COURTNEY, 13

Teenagers, especially younger teens, feel uncomfortable when they see their parents step out of their one correct role of being a mother or father. Seeing a parent dance, tell silly jokes, play around with their friends, get loud, speak in a foolish tone of voice, or behave in any way that hints of immaturity is enough to make most teens cringe.

▪ "I'm on their level. They don't want me to be on their level. They want me to be an old fart." 49-YEAR-OLD FATHER

I say, continue to enjoy yourself, but be sensitive to your teen. Although they don't always admit it, many teens find a parent with a little foolishness and fun in him is a good thing. But try to tune in to when enough is enough. I'm about as silly as they come, and I usually get away with quite a bit of joking with my daughter's friends, but I can always tell when it's going too far for her. She gives me the evil eye. I don't stop dead in my tracks, but I retreat, and I know she appreciates it.

For Divorced Parents Only

Teenagers have strong opinions on who their parents should or should not date. They say:

▪ "I feel he isn't good enough for her anyway, daughters come first." GWENDOLYN, 14

▪ "Her date was checking me out. I thought she should know what kind of a slime he was." LENA, 16

▪ "It *is* my business that my mother doesn't get hurt. *Believe me* I'm going to ask questions about it." GEORGE, 16

▪ "He had long teeth like Dracula." MARSHA, 15

▪ "My father's date was skinny and ugly, and everybody would make jokes about her." BONNIE, 13

▪ "He was so bossy and wouldn't mind his business, and this man might become my stepfather." WINSTON, 15

▪ "He's English, and he had this accent. I didn't think he was cool." PETE, 17

▪ "He was rude and obnoxious, and I told him so right to his face when my mother was there." KARA, 17

As you can see, teenagers look out for their own interests as well as yours. While they don't think anyone but their real parent is worthy of you in the first place, they also fear that your date will steal time and attention away from them. To most teens, the ultimate disaster would be that you marry someone who would steal attention away from them, and pose a threat to the image of the parent no longer living with them.

Nothing could be more humiliating or frustrating to teenagers than to see a parent going out with someone they perceive as ugly. The Dracula example may be laughable, but can be sad when you think of a teen who has images of all of her friends making fun of her mother's date, or of this horrific being actually kissing her mother. If your teenager insults your date, it's probably because she feels powerless to do anything about the dilemma she perceives herself to be in.

It would help to bring things out into the open. Help your teen to realize that her friends don't really think less of her even if her mother's date is ugly. Ask her to evaluate how she feels if she sees a friend's mother dating someone who may have major faults. Your teen will realize that since she thinks little or nothing of it, probably her friends do the same where she and her mother (and Dracula) are concerned.

But what should you do if your teen just can't stand the person you're dating? Most teens will reject anyone, no matter how perfect that person may be. Listen to your teen's opinion, but then explain that your tastes differ and this person is only a date, not a stepparent. However, if it gets serious, and the date is a potential stepparent, you'll have to remind your teen that this person doesn't want to take the place of the real parent. No one can do that anyway, but the stepparent would like to play a role in your teen's life, one that can be worked out between the two of them.

In time, many teens are able to accept the potential stepparent. Pete, for example, told me that his mother ended up marrying the man with the English accent, and they now get along just fine.

How Dare You Defy Me?

As if correcting our dress and behavior weren't enough, our teenagers also often behave as if our rules have no meaning to them. They may defy us openly and often. To most parents, defiance feels like a slap in the face. When teenagers blatantly refuse to do what they are told, parents feel:

■ "Helpless!" [when she said she would continue to see this older boy] 37-YEAR-OLD MOTHER

■ "Like finding the biggest belt and . . ." [when he talks back to me in the most insolent way] 42-YEAR-OLD FATHER

■ "Like putting her in a foster home" [after she stayed out all night]. 41-YEAR-OLD MOTHER

■ "Like she does it to hurt me" [when she comes home late time and again]. 38-YEAR-OLD MOTHER

■ "I can't handle him" [when he was punished and he took the car and went out anyway]. 45-YEAR-OLD FATHER

Why do teenagers defy their parents? Interestingly, I have found that they almost *never* do it to deliberately hurt or disrespect them. I asked teenagers to give me an example of when they openly defied their parents and to tell me why they did it. Here's what some of them said:

■ "When my mother forbid me to see my boyfriend, and kept a watch on me, I cut out of school to see him because I missed him." JODI, 17

■ "When I was 12, my parents said I was too young to have a boyfriend, but all my friends had boyfriends so I saw him in school anyway. Looking back, it was such baby stuff anyway. Big deal." TARA, 16

■ "Some boys came to our window at night to talk to me, and my father said I couldn't talk to them. As soon as he went to bed, they came back and I talked to them anyway. I think he should have at least given me a limited time to end up the conversation." CAITLIN, 16

■ "My mother never lets me out. I feel like I'm in a jail, so once in a while, I sneak out." LISANDRA, 15

■ "I stayed out late because everyone else was allowed, and I didn't want to look like a baby." TED, 15

▨ "I'm addicted to cigarettes, so I smoke behind their backs." GABRIELLE, 15

▨ "I stole the car because I thought it was worth it, even though I knew I would get caught." PETE, 17

▨ "I invited people over to the house when I was told not to because I thought I could get away with it." FRANCINE, 15

▨ "My mother said I couldn't get my hair cut short, but I had my mind set on it, so one day I just went in and got it cut. I figured, once it's done, what could they do and anyway, it's my hair, isn't it?" DONNA, 15

Often teenagers defy parents because parents ask the impossible of them. It's unrealistic to expect a teen to just stop seeing a boyfriend, or stop smoking without any help, just because you say so. If your teen's defiance is worrying you, ask yourself: "Am I making unrealistic demands?" By telling your teen that you forbid her to go out with someone, you set up a situation in which she almost *must* rebel. It would be more realistic to limit her time with him, and continue to have open conversations with her about your objections. Believe it or not, sooner or later you're bound to get through. Many teens have told me that they ended up rejecting boyfriends and girlfriends because of things their parents pointed out and they eventually agreed with (see Chapter 5 for proofs).

My own daughter is an example. She was going out with a boy who managed to upset her so much that she would scream over the phone at him and throw things around the room. He would infuriate her by not calling for days and then making up a lame excuse. I would listen to her complaints, and talk about my own experiences with guys like that. I'd let her know how lucky she'd be if she could tell, at such a young age, when a relationship isn't worth the bother, because it's a mistake to become deeply involved in a negative relationship. It's a risk at any age for one negative relationship to lead to another, and perhaps eventually to a series of them. I also made a deal with her that she could see the boy only on weekends and one day during the week, controlling my impulse to forbid her to see him at all. But I kept expressing confidence in her power to get out of a negative relationship. Sure enough, in a matter of months she broke up with him. "We have completely different values," she said. "We can't agree on anything." You can imagine how thrilled I was. Not only was the immediate problem solved, but she had learned some very important things about relationships, values, and compatibility.

Another reason a teen may defy her parents is to enjoy the pleasure of the moment. Francine wants so much to have a good time that she has her friends over despite her parents orders to the contrary. In most cases, teens hope that they won't get caught, but often, even if they know they will get caught, they commit the forbidden act anyway, anticipating the consequences later.

Teens often believe that your limits are unwarranted, unnecessary, and overcautious. Since they realize through past experience that there's no use in trying to convince you to change your mind, they take a chance and do it anyway, believing that no harm will be done. In Francine's mind, nothing bad will happen if she has friends over when you're not home. You're just a worrier from the older generation. You can't help yourself. Pete knows he won't wreck the car if he takes it out for a spin. He's a careful driver. Everyone in the driver's ed class knows *that*.

Most teens don't defy you to hurt or disrespect you—they just want to enjoy their lives. Should you let them get away with it? Of course not. You should talk it out. If you really want to solve the problem, in most cases, you'll have to do a little compromising. When you give a little and take a little with teenagers, they try to keep up their end of the bargain, because they perceive themselves as being respected.

But don't expect miracles overnight. Realize that teens will try to get away with something. And what's more, if you find out your teen is breaking the bargain, don't fall into the trap of taking it as a personal insult. For example, if you find that your daughter is seeing a boy more often than she agreed upon, rather than pounce on her and say, "How could you betray me?" realize that it's hard for a teen who thinks she's in love to resist the temptation to see her boyfriend every day. Instead, tell her that you know she's been seeing him more than you had agreed, and although you know how tempting it is to cheat, a bargain is a bargain. Try to get her to go along with you because of her own sense of honor rather than because she fears your wrath or she feels she's betraying you if she breaks the agreement. The sense-of-honor concept is strongest because if she violates it, she feels she is betraying *herself*. When she keeps it, she's honoring her own integrity.

Don't Believe That Hard Exterior

When you have a terrible fight with your teenager, you may think it doesn't faze him or her, because teenagers often wear a mask of indifference to hide what they're really feeling. But when teenagers have a fight with their parents, they tell me:

■ "I'm depressed all day in school. I feel guilty because she is my mother and I don't want to hurt her. I feel really bad, like the whole world has ended, but she doesn't know." LOUISE, 15

■ "I feel like everything she said about me is true. I feel hurt and alone. I think maybe she doesn't love me." NATALIE, 16

■ "I think of throwing myself out of the window or poisoning myself. I say, 'What's the use of living if nobody cares?'" MIMI, 18

■ "When she's yelling at me I look all evil and I ignore her, but what she doesn't know is when I say 'I hate you,' it really means 'I love you.'" SHARELL, 16

■ "When my mother fights with me, she criticizes and ridicules me. Later I think she must really think badly of me." MARNIE, 17

■ "I feel hurt inside like my insides just left me but I never let her know it." SEAN, 17

■ "I feel like taking all my things and staying away for a few weeks, and letting them get really scared." KENT, 16

■ "I feel sad and heartbroken like I'm drained all the way down to the bottom." BRANDY, 18

Do their parents know the way they feel? Almost never! I asked hundreds of teens if they tell their parents how bad they feel after a fight, and all admit they never talk about it. Most of them say they don't bring up the subject of their sorrow over the argument because they fear that the argument itself will begin again.

I used to be quick with my tongue toward my own daughter, but one day I learned I must use more self-control. I was screaming at her because her face showed no indication that I was getting through to her; she suddenly started sobbing as if her heart would break. I was so shocked that I stopped in the middle of my tirade. I put my arms around her and told her that I loved her. I then explained that I never dreamed she was feeling any-thing because her face appeared cold and hard, and I thought she was being defiant. After a long talk, I found out that many times in the past, she had been deeply hurt by my rage and my words, but had never let me know. Where had she learned to cover her emotions? Obviously not from me. I would like to blame her painful reticence on my ex-husband, because he used to say, "Stop crying or I'll give you something to cry about." Nevertheless, the thing to do, clearly, was to change things *immediately*. From that day on, I was more sensitive to my daughter's feelings.

The Worst Thing You Ever Said to Your Teenager

Parents are surprised when they find out that they have said extremely cruel things to their teens. I asked teenagers to tell me the worst thing their parents ever said to them. Here they are in order of the most repeated:

▨ "I can't wait until you're out of this house."
▨ "I wish you were never born."
▨ "You're going to be a big zero!"
▨ "I hate you."
▨ "I'm sending you to live with your father."

Some parents add details, such as "I'm counting the days until you leave," "You ruined my life," "You're a loser," "I wish you were dead," or "I'm packing your bags right now." What kind of parents would say such things? Self-centered parents? Emotionally immature parents? Child abusers? Yes—and most normal parents, too! Who among us has not said something horrible to our teen in a moment of anger?

If you are guilty of saying unkind things, I have a perfect remedy, and it works every time. *Apologize.* Go to your teen and tell the truth exactly as you feel it: "I'm really sorry I said I hate you. I don't hate you. I love you. I hate what you do sometimes, because I feel frustrated, and I can't cope. Sometimes I want to run away from it all myself. Sometimes I wish I could just take a trip around the world and forget all my troubles. But I can't. I know it's not your fault. Of course I do." (Don't be embarrassed to cry if you feel like it.) Then put your arms around your teen and give him or her a big hug. You'll be amazed to find out that your teen will understand. You'll make your teen feel so good inside, you'll see an immediate change in the expression on his or her face. Swallow your pride and apologize.

But what if you find yourself apologizing all the time? So what? Better to apologize a thousand times than to let one poisonous remark remain without an antidote. Your apology means everything. And you're setting an example to your teen that it's not a weakness to apologize. And what's more, after a while, you'll find yourself curbing your tongue when you're about to get vicious. For some reason, your past, loving apologies will help you to control yourself. You'll see. It really works.

Apologizing also helps you to have a closer, more open relationship with your teen, because a special love passes between you two when you're being that honest.

When Teenagers Feel Sorry for Their Parents

Teenagers are more softhearted and mature than we realize. I asked teens if they ever felt sorry for their parents. Teens say:

■ "I feel sorry for my mother when my brother gives her a hard time." CHRISTINE, 17

■ "When my father looks depressed about paying the bills, and he talks about working overtime, I think he's getting old and he shouldn't have to work so much." SHELLEY, 15

■ "When my father had to get a tumor removed, he looked scared. It bothered me to see him look that way." SAL, 18

■ "When my mother lost her gold and diamond heart necklace she was almost crying." EVE, 13

■ "When my mother is planning to do something exciting and she's not able to, I think she has a hard life." TONETTE, 17

■ "My father is not working now, and he looks sad. I feel so sorry for him." NAOMI, 16

■ "My mother is physically fit, and when she was young she was a good gymnast, but in Trinidad there wasn't such a thing as the Olympics. Her talent went to waste." MONICA, 15

■ "When my mother didn't get the job she interviewed for, she walked slowly into the house and put her head on the table. She looked so depressed." DENNIS, 14

■ "My mother and I were in the store, and she was buying

me all these very expensive clothes. She works hard for her money, and I felt selfish taking the clothes. I felt like I don't deserve it. I love her." MARTINA, 16

■ "When I had to leave my dad on the weekend. His eyes looked watery." PAULIE, 13

■ "Whenever my mother sees my dad and his new family, because my dad left my mother for another woman, and now they have a child together." KIM, 16

■ "When she came home from work and looked tired, and had to clean the house." ROSEANNE, 17

■ "When she's fed up with work, rent, and how expensive it is to live in the city." MARK, 15

If teens share their parents' pain, why don't they let their parents know it? When I ask them, their universal answer is, "I feel stupid."

How can you get your teen to express his or her compassion? It's easy. Here's a golden opportunity to talk to your teen as an equal. Start a conversation about what's bothering you. Be honest and open about your feelings, just the way you would be with an adult friend. I did it all the time with my daughter, and before I knew it, she would be comforting me. It was heartening and rather funny, because these are the times I would see my own philosophy coming back to me through my daughter. She would say something like, "Don't worry, Mom. In the long run, it will work out. It always does." Cheered not only that she showed such empathy, but that she's picked up my positive outlook, I would say something like: "You're right. I know that, but sometimes I just get a little tired." Then she would say, "I know what you mean!" and we would feel a special closeness at that moment.

As such hard-earned moments of closeness accumulate, they contribute enormously toward building and cementing a durable, loving, open parent-teen relationship. Since troubled times can provide the opportunity to build better relationships, we should take full advantage of them.

But Dad, I Know More about This Than You Do

Your suspicions are right. In her heart of hearts, your teenager believes she knows more than you do. In his innermost being, your teenager feels that he must correct your thinking. Exactly why do teenagers feel this way?

▪ "Since my brain is young, and my parents' brains are old, I can learn and understand more things in general." HOPE, 16

▪ "Parents are older and they get nervous about things and tend to overreact. We have to calm them down." KIRK, 17

▪ "They are thinking from the past rather than what's happening now so it's a big job to educate them on reality today." SADIE, 15

▪ "I think I know more about sex and standards with teens than my parents. They remember rules from years ago, but things have changed drastically. The game has changed, and teens play by different rules." JULIETTE, 16

▪ "It doesn't matter if I'm the child and they're the parents. If our opinions or thinking differ, we should express it. They may see our side of it and learn from it. That's the only way to have a close relationship." MATTI, 15

■ "I've been around long enough to see my parents make many mistakes, so if I see them about to make another one, I figure I have to warn them." DEMETREUS, 19

■ "We learn more in school than they did. For example, I'm better in math than my parents, and I read more than they do. I know things they are unfamiliar with." JUSTINE, 17

■ "I'm better at organizing things than my mother." AUDRA, 13

■ "I tell my mother how to handle my stepfather, and I tell my stepfather how to handle my mother, because I see what's going on between them, and I know how to fix it. Sometimes they tell me I'm a natural psychologist." SELINA, 15

Let's educate Hope: Senility does not set in during the thirties or forties. Kirk, however, has a point: Sometimes parents of teens overreact. Maybe you haven't yet let your sagacious teen teach you that; maybe, on the other hand, you learned it years earlier through raising more than one teen and you now save your energy for the *big* issues. Maybe you'll even experience flashes of how smart you (the parent) were when you were a teen. Sadie and Martelle are also right, in a way: Teens do have a job to educate us to what is happening in their teen world. I remember having to forever ask my daughter and other teenagers for intelligence on the latest language, dress, hairstyles, music, and other fast-forward teen topics. I would also ask about more sensitive issues, like whether or not most teens today are having sex, or whether most teens smoke marijuana or do other drugs.

As parents, we have life experience. But before we share it with them, we have to show appreciation for their life experience, too, and take it into consideration. Then they're more likely to believe we know what we're talking about.

Mattie and Demetreus realize that parents are only human and make mistakes, and that even though they are still teenagers, some of their ideas may be helpful. I would ask my daughter's opinion, and see her brow furrow as she thought of the best advice she could give me. Sometimes it was excellent, and I followed it. Other times, wisely, I thanked her but didn't follow it. But I made her feel important anyway. I showed her the respect she deserved, found out how she felt, got a second opinion, and in the bargain, set an example. I want her to ask for my opinion when something comes up in her life. To this day we ask and value each other's opinions.

Justine points out the simple fact that some teens are better educated than their parents in certain academic areas. If that's true of your teen, take advantage of the fact, and let him or her teach you a thing or two. Wherever you're quite content to let your teen be the expert, you'll find it natural to express pleasure in his or her standing. After all, the teen is your child.

Audra and Selina point out the factor of innate talent. Evidently Audra is more gifted than her mother in organizing, and Selina is, as her parents put it, a natural psychologist. When you find that your teen is gifted in areas where you're not, appreciate your differences in talent. You can encourage the talent and help build self-esteem, and at the same time you can help your teen to see that you recognize that he or she is an individual, separate and apart from you. That support will help your teen to continue to grow and develop a distinct talent and personality without guilt. Teens don't want to feel as if they are carbon copies of their parents. If we let our children be individuals, sooner or later they will find things in themselves that remind them of their parents, and will enjoy claiming them: "I have my mother's sense of humor" or "I have my father's determination."

Reminders

1. Teenagers correct our dress, hair, makeup, and behavior because they think they are protecting us from making fools of ourselves.

2. Teens get embarrassed when parents step out of line and don't appear motherly or fatherly. They feel most comfortable with parents who are somewhere in the middle, neither ultra-hip nor too old-fashioned; and anything that hints of silliness or sexuality in their parents makes teens cringe.

3. Don't drastically change your dress, hair, makeup, or behavior to accommodate teens, but do be sensitive to their feelings and open to modifying your style at times.

4. To help your teen to not defy you, evaluate your demands. If you are asking the impossible, find a way to compromise.

5. Don't take defiance personally. Teens are not thinking: "I will disrespect my mother and do this." Most of the time they defy you because they want to do what they want to do, and believe they will not get caught. They reason that there's no harm in the activity; or they get

caught up in the pleasure of the moment and brush aside all thoughts of the consequences.

6. Don't believe that hard exterior. When you have a fight with your teen, you may think it's left him unfazed because he wears a protective mask of indifference. Inside your teen's feeling hurt, alone, upset, perhaps even crushed.

7. Teens don't usually tell you how hurt they feel after a fight because they're afraid to open up the whole can of worms again. If you've had a fight with your teen, even if he or she was at fault, make the first move. Give your teen a hug and tell him you love him. While he's pushing you away, he's storing away the love he desperately needs.

8. If you have said horrible things to your teen, welcome to the club. Instead of berating yourself, apologize—it's always better late than never—and explain as best you can what was going through your mind at the moment, and what you believe *really* was responsible for your outburst. Such conversations will bring love and healing to you and your teen and create permanent bonds. It's better to have to apologize a thousand times than to let one poisonous remark remain without antidote.

9. Ask your teenager for information about her interests, and ask her opinion whenever possible. You'll learn a lot about the way she thinks, and you'll be teaching her to ask your opinion too.

10. Talent knows no age limit. Your teenager surely excels in certain areas where you don't. Celebrate your teen's strengths. It will help your teen to find his or her identity and to build self-esteem.

Chapter 5

Those So-Called Friends Are Bad News

One of the greatest fears parents have is that their teenagers will be influenced by the wrong crowd. Parents worry that the more they try to influence their teen to stay away from a certain friend, the more likely their teen is to rebel and hang around with that friend. Parents say:

- "You usually do what your friends are doing."
- "I told you he was trouble."
- "Just being with them is bad judgment."

This chapter contains good news. You will find out how teens are influenced by their parents' lectures about friends and why teens rarely tell their parents they were right about a certain friend, even though they eventually drop the friend in question. You will also be able to put things into perspective by taking a trip down memory lane regarding some of your own friends when you were a teen, and why they did or did not have a long-term influence on you.

In addition, you will find out how teens feel when parents step out of bounds and scold, insult, or otherwise mistreat friends, and you will discover ways to repair the damage if you have made mistakes in dealing with your teenager and his or her friends.

Friends Parents Dislike

When I ask parents to characterize dubious friends of their teens, I get answers like these: a beer-drinking, pot-smoking partygoer; a foulmouthed loser; a self-centered, disrespectful, arrogant airhead; a suggestive dresser; a vicious troublemaker. Have you found yourself trying desperately to protect your teenager from the influence of any of these? Teenagers complain:

■ "My mother called my best friend a whore, and said if I didn't watch out, I'd end up just like her." CATHY, 14

■ "Just because my friend was engaged when she was 16, my father does not want me to hang around with her. He says: She knows too much for her age." DARA, 15

■ "My parents say my friend brings out the crazy, mischievous side of me. They say he's trouble, then they bring up something he did that wasn't kosher." JASON, 19

■ "I always get in trouble when I'm with Sheena, so my mother says she's a bad influence." REBECCA, 15

■ "My father doesn't like me hanging out with Marlene, because she's disrespectful to people. He says it's rubbing off on me." TANYA, 14

■ "My parents can't stand Rob just because he's failing every subject in school. They say: 'Before you know it, you'll be cutting classes, too.'" TOM, 15

Parents warn, and teens don't like it. But do parents' words go unheeded? Is it all a waste of time? Be ready for some surprises.

Can Parents Influence Their Teen's Choice of Friends?

Though teenagers generally hate to admit it they really do hear what their parents tell them. Here's what teens say:

■ "When my friend Jackie would tell me to cut school, I would think of my mother saying she is trouble, and I would feel very uncomfortable. I'd end up not having a good time when I cut, and I eventually stopped hanging out with her." RACHEL, 13

■ "My mother told me my friend envied me, and she turned out to be right. She was spreading rumors about me behind my back, and I found out about it." KIMBERLY, 14

■ "My parents warned me about the guys that hang around the poolroom, and sure enough, every one of them is either on drugs or involved in some illegal activity. I finally moved on to another crowd." QUENTIN, 18

■ "I remember a time when my friend wanted me to go with her to this bad neighborhood to see her boyfriend, but I heard my mother's nagging in the back of my mind, and I didn't go." ANITA, 16

■ "When I went to a carnival with my friend, and she started talking to all these guys, and leaning up against them and acting—you know—my mother's words came back to me. I didn't want people to think I was just like her." SADIE, 15

■ "My parents told me that Cookie was totally self-centered, and that I was starting to act just like her. Then one night I slept over at her house, and she had such a nasty attitude with her mother because her mother didn't buy her anything. I thought she was being so selfish, and I thought about what my parents said." JANNA, 16

■ "I usually realize my parents were right after something happens to prove them right. Yet when they try to warn me about something, I tell them they don't know what they're talking about." VAN, 17

Most teenagers *are* affected by their parents' warnings. But do they usually give parents the satisfaction of knowing that they are right? Of course not.

Do Teenagers Ever Admit You Were Right?

I asked teenagers: "Did you ever tell your parents that they were right, or did you just keep it to yourself?" Teens say:

■ "No. I would never do that." KATY, 13

■ "I keep it to myself. If I told them, my parents would be so stuck-up afterwards." LORI, 14

■ "I don't tell them because I'll never hear the end of it." EUGENIA, 16

■ "If I tell my father he's right, he'll *always* think he's right." CAL, 17

■ "If I told them they were right, the next thing you know they'd be trying to tell me how to run my life every minute of the day." TONY, 15

■ "I don't tell them because I don't want to hear, 'I told you so.'" DALLA, 16

▪ "I kept it to myself. I didn't think it was important to tell them." JILLIAN, 15

▪ "I didn't want to open up the whole can of worms again!" WILLIE, 19

▪ "I didn't want him to have the satisfaction of being right." JOHN, 17

▪ "I didn't want to give them any recognition." CHRISSY, 17

▪ "It was too embarrassing to tell them." KAREN, 13

Apparently, teens would like to tell their parents that they were right, but they dread hearing "I told you so," or a speech about how parents always know best. What's more, they fear that their parents would take such an admission as their license for controlling their teens' future activities. So rather than take the chance, most teenagers keep the knowledge stored away in their own minds.

Some, however, do tell their parents they were right. Here's why:

▪ "I told my mother she was right because I felt I owed her that much. I wanted to give credit where credit was due." PENNY, 15

▪ "I tell her because she never lectures me, but acts proud, and it seems like she thinks I've learned from my mistakes." EILEEN, 16

▪ "I tell them because I want to confirm their ideas and opinions. I'd want someone to do the same for me." JASON, 19

Apparently, the best way to encourage your teen to let you know that your ideas and values are getting through is to refrain from taking the credit in the first place, and to convey instead that you're delighted to see how mature your teen is becoming and how much he or she is learning about life. If we can resist the temptation to extol our own wisdom, and let our teens talk about the lessons they have learned, we will find them coming back again and again with news of how right we were about various things.

But even if you don't ever get to hear from your teen that you were right, and that you did have an effect upon your teen's choice of friends (or other things, for that matter), don't be discouraged. Isn't it true that, to this day, there are things you decided your parents were right about and you never told them? The point is, don't yield to the temptation to stop expressing your opinion and your concern. Believe it or not, it is sinking in.

Teenagers Wouldn't Let Their Children Hang Around With . . .

Even as teenagers are fighting you every step of the way about the friends you dislike, they're surprisingly conservative when asked what types of friends they would want their own teenagers to hang around with. Teens say they would forbid their own teens to associate with:

■ "Someone who cuts school or does drugs." CHARITY, 14
■ "Lowlifes with a bad reputation." GRETA, 17

▨ "Kids who are always in the street." MARY, 15

▨ "A person who has no respect for their parents." GUY, 18

▨ "Anyone who steals or lies a lot." AUGUSTA, 13

▨ "Girls who are loud or loose." RENE, 16

▨ "A person with a weak family background." VITO, 19

The fact that teens say such things is an indication that they're internalizing their parents' values. Find out if your teen's been absorbing your values by asking him or her the same question. But make sure you ask in a conversational, just-for-fun way rather than one that says, "See? You'll feel the same way I do when you're a parent."

Never, Never Do or Say That to My Friend Again

We've already looked at teens' complaints about embarrassing parental behavior. But there are certain things teens feel parents should *never* say or do to their friends. I asked teenagers: "What is the worst thing your parents ever said or did to one of your friends?"

▨ "My mother told my friends that when I was little I was watching this dog urinate, and that's how I first noticed the color yellow. It's such a stupid story, and when she does it, I say, 'Oh no, not again.' I spoke to her about it." TIMMY, 15

▨ "My mother showed my friend my fifth-grade picture and I looked terrible. I felt like snatching it out of her hand and ripping it up." WESTON, 17

▨ "One day this girl, not a girlfriend, just a girl whose

friend was at the house, and me, we were talking. My mother yells, 'Sherman, wash the dishes,' and I pretended like I didn't hear her. A few minutes later she comes in and says: 'Get your butt in the kitchen and wash the dishes. How many times do I have to tell you? You think you're grown, but I've got news for you.' I was so ashamed, I felt like cursing my mother and running out of the house." SHERMAN, 15

■ "My mother told my girlfriend that her skirt was too short. She said, 'I'm only telling you for your own good.' I thought, 'Mind your own damn business, Mom.' Her mother doesn't tell me how to dress. I felt like apologizing to my friend for my mother. My friend looked ashamed and embarrassed." ANASTASIA, 16

■ "My father told my friend he was immature and didn't know left from right. I was embarrassed, and wondered if my friend would take it out on me." MONTE, 14

■ "When this guy called me, my father asked him why he was calling. I thought it wasn't necessary to give guys the third degree, and I wanted to cry." LINA, 14

■ "My mother told this guy that I really wanted to speak to that I wasn't home. I was furious, and I asked her how could she do a thing like that. I was in a rage all night." BELINDA, 16

■ "I came home late one night with my girlfriend, and my mother started screaming that it was my girlfriend's influence because her parents let her be irresponsible and have a late curfew. She then insulted my girlfriend's parents and the way they handled her. My friend was upstairs and heard everything. I was so embarrassed. I wanted to slam my mother's mouth shut. I couldn't believe she didn't have the common sense to speak to me in private about my girlfriend's influence." MARTINA, 16

■ "When my mother smacked my face in front of my friend, I said to myself, 'I don't believe she just did that.' I looked at her like she was crazy, and later I asked her if she was." CLAIRE, 14

■ "My mother said to my date, jokingly, 'Don't get her pregnant.' I think my face turned beet red at that moment. I wanted to crawl through a crack and disappear." SHARON, 17

■ "My mother started flirting with one of my guy friends. I was thinking, 'Ma, stop it. You look stupid.' I didn't say anything to her because I was too shocked and ashamed to say a word." DAISY, 14

It can be tempting to say or do anything we please when our teenager's friends are around but we must resist. Teenagers do not appreciate their parents discussing how they behaved when they were young, what they looked like, or how their friends should act, look like, or behave while they are present. The *last* thing they want to hear is anything even remotely connected to a time when they were babies. Possibly the very worst thing parents can do is to yell at their teen in front of a friend and make a comment about the teen not being physically or emotionally mature. Comments such as "You're still not grown" are very embarrassing and are likely to provoke rage.

Timmy and Weston are right to be embarrassed, and their mothers should learn that what is cute to them should be saved for sharing with other relatives or friends when the teen is *not* around. How Timmy learned to distinguish the color yellow may be absolutely adorable to his mother, but to his friends, it's ammunition for teasing, and so is Weston's childhood picture.

Sherman's rage is understandable. In his eyes his mother committed a triple crime: Not only did she embarrass him, but she did it in front of the opposite sex, and she treated him like a baby, too. Teenage boys are trying very hard to become men, and the last thing they need is to see themselves reduced to little boys by a thoughtless comment from a parent.

We as parents must work toward exercising a lot of self-control. No matter how angry you are, or how funny you think your comment will be, hold it for a moment. Stop and put yourself in your teen's shoes. Bring yourself back to that age, take into account your teen's particular personality, and imagine exactly how you would feel if those words were said to you in front of your friend. If you do this, I can practically guarantee you won't have a whole lot of trouble controlling your next impulse to say something inappropriate in your teen's eyes.

Teenagers don't appreciate it when we try to parent their friends and offer unsolicited advice. When we correct the dress or behavior of our teens' friends, our teens feel embarrassed and obligated to apologize for our indiscretion. At the same time, they feel guilty for apologizing for us, because they feel they are putting us down to their friends, admitting that something is wrong with us. True, teens will often complain to friends about the way parents treat them, and say things like "My mother is a nag," or "My father is worse than a cop," but this kind of criticism of parents doesn't count as a put-down. In fact, it says "My parents care about me." But *really* having to criticize parents to a friend is something entirely different. When a teen is forced to do this, in the teen's mind, he or she is saying "My parents don't know what they are doing, and I'm ashamed of their behavior."

What should you do if you see a blatant fault in your teen's friend? Either find a loving, positive way to point out the fault indirectly, or say nothing at all. For example, Anastasia's mother could have said something like, "What a beautiful skirt, and how lovely you look in it. It compliments your figure. If only it were a bit longer, I think it would be perfect." Another alternative is to talk to your teen about her friend's fault privately but even then, the parent should preface the criticism with a positive comment about the friend.

It's rude for parents to grill friends about the purpose of a call before handing the phone to their teen; Lina was right to be upset. However hard it may be, parents need to learn that all the grilling in the world won't uncover the subtle and intricate details of teenagers' lives. (After all, is the boy going to say "I'm calling to see if I can get your daughter to go out with me on Saturday night"? Much less will he add "And my real goal is to get her into bed.") He's going to have to make something up that he feels a parent might want to hear. The only thing you'll accomplish by grilling your teenager's friends is to afflict your teen with resentment and stress. If you want to know the purpose of the call, it's much better to ask your teen later, in the most positive, friendly way possible. Then you have a chance of getting the details if your teen is in the mood to talk, and feels he or she can trust you well enough to tell you. (See Chapter 9 for a discussion of getting your teen to tell you more details about his or her life.) Or, you can always commit the unpardonable sin and keep your ear glued to the door. I confess I've done it. But I got only half the story, and caused myself more anxiety than relief. I also felt guilty.

Like Belinda's mother, I once lied and told a guy who called that my daughter wasn't home. I resented the fact that he always called her when she was tranquilly doing her homework. I just didn't want to disturb her. Later that night he called again, and she found out about my deception. She was furious and crushed. How could I do such a thing? Did I have no sense of integrity? And she was right. I should have instead kept him on the line a moment while I told my daughter he was on the phone and that she could only talk two minutes. That may have raised a protest, but the price would have been less dear than her wondering if she could *ever* trust me to tell her if anyone called.

In addition, by lying to her, I was giving my daughter the unspoken message that lying is a legitimate way to avoid confrontations—the exact opposite of the message I would have wanted to convey to her. What's more, I was indicating that I was willing to resort to any means to regain the control I had over her when she was five years old.

I ended up admitting I was wrong and promised never to do it again. I kept the promise (and keep it yet).

Parents are all too human. If you've seriously insulted one of your teen's friends, talk to your teen and the friend about it, explaining honestly why you spoke that way, and apologize. Your teen will see that your words are sincere, and will forgive you. Martina's mother, for example, could make things right by apologizing. By the time the two girls pranced in late, she was evidently so angry that she was unable to control her temper. Apparently, Martina is not usually late, and her mother had been stewing for an hour, blaming the friend's bad influence for the lateness. By the time the girls walked in, the mother may have wanted to tell the friend off outright and give her daughter a really major tongue-lashing. In a misdirected effort at self-control, she instead blurted out insults about the friend's family not caring, and perhaps (on an unconscious level) even hoped, that the friend would hear.

In apologizing, she could explain to the girls that she was worried and building up a case against the friend because her mother allows her a later curfew. She could then explain how frustrating it was for her to be the only parent holding the line, when all others are so lenient. She could even say something like: "I feel so frustrated because there's no way I can control other parents. I know it's ridiculous, but that's how I feel." Then she could say to Martina's friend, "I'm sorry if I hurt your feelings. I have no right to judge your parents. They are fine people. I was just so frustrated." Whether or not Martina will be penalized for her lateness should, of course, be dealt with, but at another time, in private.

By the teen years, if not before, parents must face it: spanking is over. But some parents, being fallible, will, out of sheer frustration, take a swat at a teen. It's bad enough when that happens in private, but when it occurs in public, the hurt is magnified a thousand times. Truly, the offense is never justifiable in the teen's mind, and the teen says, as Claire did: "She must be crazy." If you've done something like this, try to trace the same mental pattern in your apology as Martina's mother did. Tell your teen by way of explanation, not justification, what thoughts led up to the slap. Then apologize, give her a big hug and a kiss, and tell her you love her. She'll feel it down to her soul, and the two of you may end up getting even closer than you were before the incident.

Why should I go to all this trouble? you may ask. You should do it because every hurtful action that's not discussed serves to permanently widen the rift between the parent and the teen and can eventually result in much more than a communication gap. It can end up becoming a gulf that separates so many adults from their parents for life, or at least until years of therapy have helped them to forgive their parents. It's much easier to express our sincere apologies now, when they can do the most good, than to wait until years later, when things have crystallized into permanent resentment.

Sharon's mother was joking, but not joking, when she told Sharon's date not to get her pregnant. She was really expressing her fears out loud. Teenagers are already uneasy about their sexuality, and the last thing they need is to hear the subject brought into the open with a joke in front of a teen of the opposite sex. The remark was completely inappropriate, and Sharon's mother should give a sincere apology with a simple explanation: "I'm sorry I said that. It was a stupid thing to say. I thought I was being funny, but no sooner did the words come out of my mouth than I realized how ridiculous I sounded but it was too late." If Sharon said something like: "But you *always* try like that to be funny, Mom," her mother could respond: "You're right. I do it too often. I think I'll have to put a muzzle on when your friends are around." Sharon will soften, and probably laugh. Most teens are much more resilient than we imagine, if given even a reasonable amount of respect and understanding.

As tempting as it may be, parents have to control their impulse to flirt with their teenagers' friends. It's normal for parents to note the attractiveness of their teens' friends of the opposite sex, and to behave foolishly around them without realizing it. If you do that or have done it, forgive yourself for being human, but resolve to maintain a friendly but more parental stance where your teen's friends are concerned. If you flirt with them, or encourage them when they flirt with you, at best you look foolish, and at worst, you appear desperate. You can get your kicks elsewhere. The momentary exhilaration is not worth the price of humiliation and confusion to your teen. If you must flirt with the younger generation, no one is stopping you from batting your eyelashes at the supermarket clerk or the usher at the movies, or chatting with the boys at the beach when your teen is not around.

Boyfriends and Girlfriends You Don't Trust

Most parents have had the experience of seeing their teenager go out with someone they disapprove of. Is there any use in talking to them about it? Do our warnings serve to make them go only more deeply into the relationship? A pleasant surprise awaits you.

▓ "This girl named Lisa was trying to use me, and my mother told me I was looking at her through rose-colored glasses. Later I found out she was using me to death." RONALD, 17

■ "When I was going out with Dave, my mother kept telling me something was wrong with our relationship, because he got me upset all the time. She would say, 'If you two were compatible, you wouldn't be crying all the time.' She was so right. Hopefully I'll never get myself into something like that again." KIAH, 16

■ "My father warned me that Rene was a hoodlum, but I just laughed it off. But then I thought about it, and it was true. What did he have going for him? All he did was hang out with his friends; he had no goal, no job, and he did drugs once in awhile. I think I lost respect for him or something, because eventually he started to turn me off." BARBARA, 18

When it comes to the opposite sex, I'm not of the laissez-faire school. While I don't believe we can get away with just laying down the law, "I forbid you to do that or else" (it wouldn't work anyway, they would just sneak around), I do think we owe it to our teens to exert a heavy influence when we perceive that they are in a potentially harmful relationship.

We can do a few things. We can limit their time with the individual, and we can talk and keep on talking. Your teen won't let you know it at the time, but as you can see from the earlier quotes, your lectures are permanently recorded and they play back in your teen's mind at just the right moments. Barbara's father's speeches came back to her from time to time when she observed certain behavior in Rene, and those replays helped her to come to the conclusion that Rene was not right for her.

Do you think all the teens I've just quoted went running back to their parents to tell them that they were right? Of course they didn't. Most of them kept it to themselves. So let that be a lesson to you. Your lectures are not going unheard and most likely they're not going unheeded.

All Your Friends Were Perfect!

Parents are very idealistic when it comes to the kinds of friends they want their teenagers to have. When asked to describe the perfect friend for their teen, parents said things like: responsible; friendly; good moral values, like Jesus; someone who respects authority; intelligent; loves school; plans to go to college; doesn't swear, drink, or do drugs; well-mannered, quiet, industrious, and has goals.

Yet when asked to describe some of the friends they had when they were teens, parents realized, generally with surprise, that often their friends were quite unlike the ideal friends they have in mind for their teens.

I asked parents to describe a friend they had as a teen, one they would never want their own teen to hang out with. I also asked what influence that friend had upon them. Parents said:

▪ "I had a friend who was very violent and went out of his way to look for trouble. He ended up in jail but I ended up going to college." 37-YEAR-OLD FATHER

▪ "One of my girlfriends was kind of a slut. But she did what she was going to do, and I did what I was going to do. Neither one of us influenced the other. I don't know what happened to her, because after high school, I lost touch with her." 46-YEAR-OLD MOTHER

■ "My girlfriend was disrespectful to her parents. She ran wild. I think she made me love my parents more, not less, and I remember I felt sorry for her parents." 39-YEAR-OLD MOTHER

■ "My friend did drugs, but he didn't have any influence on me. He was a heavy user. For all I know, he OD'd or ended up on skid row." 36-YEAR-OLD FATHER

■ "My bad friend was more influenced by me than I was by her." 40-YEAR-OLD MOTHER

■ "I had this friend who was very prejudiced and said hateful things toward others. I remember thinking that his parents must have brought him up that way and at a certain point, I decided not to be friends with him anymore." 47-YEAR-OLD FATHER

Interesting, isn't it? Think back to your own teen years. Can you recall one particular friend that you would never want your teen to hang around with? Did that friend affect the direction of your life? From what I gather, if there's a strong family influence, it's highly likely that the friend can effect only a minor or temporary negative influence. In the long run, solid values instilled by parents win out even if there are some wanderings. In fact, in the long run, you may find that your offspring chooses friends who confirm his or her family's good example. I'm reminded of the biblical proverb that my own mother would quote to me, time and again:

> *Train up a child in the way he should go: and when he is old, he will not depart from it.*
> (Prov. 22:6, King James Version)

Notice, the proverb wisely qualified the promise: when he is old or when he matures. There will be times when you'll wonder if you're wasting your energy. But as one father says:

▪ "We brought him up right, gave him lots of love, and always had a close-knit family. When we found out he was involved in drugs, we were heartbroken. We had to put him in a drug rehabilitation program in Minnesota. I remember feeling like a failure as we flew down to the place. But now he's 25, has a good job with a construction company, and is engaged to be married. And the funny thing is, he's now more conservative than I am in some ways." 52-YEAR-OLD FATHER

Keep on doing your job. Unlikely though it may seem, your teen will come around.

Reminders

1. Even though your teen may argue, he or she will seriously consider your comments about your teen's choice of friends.
2. If you generally resist the temptation to say "I told you so," and instead let your teen believe she has discovered a truth for herself, she'll be more likely to let you know that you were right about certain friends.
3. Teenagers are surprisingly conservative when it comes to deciding what kinds of friends they, as parents, would let their own teenagers have. That's one very strong indication that most teens are absorbing their parents' values after all.

4. Teens don't like parents to talk about their infancy or child-hood in front of their friends. Sharing their cute-kid tricks or hauling out their old photos will embarrass your teen.

5. When we scold or correct our teens' friends, we cause our teenagers great embarrassment, and we put them in the position of having to apologize for us. They end up feeling guilty and angry at the same time.

6. Avoid the temptation to grill telephone callers on the nature of their business with your teen. You're unlikely to get true information; you *are* likely to invoke stress, distrust, and resentment in your teen.

7. If you can't stand your teen's boyfriend or girlfriend, keep talking about it (whether or not your audience seems to be listening). In time, your teen will probably realize that what you have been saying is true.

8. If you've embarrassed your teen by stepping out of line with a friend, apologize to your teen *and* the friend. Let them know what forces and thought process caused the insult.

9. Many parents who counted some sketchy people among their friends when they were teens feel that it was their parents' influence, and not the influence of the those particular friends, who determined their values and actions. This should be encouraging for you.

10. If your teenager seems to be a hopeless case at 17, wait awhile. When your teen reaches 25, he or she may be more conservative than you are.

Chapter 6
Things That Drive You Up the Wall

Most teenagers have the power to make even a saint curse. Do they plan to drive you crazy, or it is just their instinctive talent?

■ "Is this the same human being that came out of my womb?" 40-YEAR-OLD MOTHER

What bothers one parent may not bother another, but chances are you'll find that some things in this chapter will strike a familiar chord. They play their music loud, no matter how many times you ask them to turn it down; they monopolize the telephone; snap their gum; borrow your shampoo; steal your clothing; use abusive, annoying, or foul language; refuse to cut their hair; and roll their eyes. The list goes on and on.

When my daughter was a toddler, and all her friends were between the ages of three and five, I clearly remember wondering: "Can children play without shrieking? Can they learn to lower their voices?" Realizing that trying to lower their volume would be fighting a ridiculous and losing battle, I, of course, made no attempt to convince my 4-year-old and her friends that they should speak in soft tones. It seemed to be natural for them to scream. We've all gone through it and we're only too happy when *that* phase is over.

Turn Down That Music

For teens, is playing loud music a necessary expression of the joy of living? Is there some hidden need that teenagers have, despite the invention of headphones, that compels them to blast their stereos for all the world to hear (until it goes deaf)? I asked teenagers why they play their music loud, even though they know it annoys their parents. They say:

▨ "Because it puts me in a good mood to hear a cool song loud. I don't do it to spite my parents. I just forget." TRACY, 16

▨ "It's the only way I can relax." KAREN, 17

▨ "Some records have a nice beat, so when they come on, I just get crazy and turn up the volume." PERRY, 15

▨ "Because I like it loud, and if I play it soft, they complain anyway, so what the hell." LAURON, 14

▨ "Because that's the only way to listen to hip-hop." DARYL, 18

▨ "Puts me in a good mood, relaxes me, makes me happy." TINA, 16

I asked thousands of teens who said the same thing: In essence, they use the music as a harmless outlet, a vehicle for escaping from their woes, however briefly.

It would be ideal to provide them with a time and place where they can blast their music as loud as they please and not disturb anybody. Most likely, they find such places anyway (driving in cars with other teens, in the schoolyard, at the beach). When they don't, they stay home and serenade themselves and you. Teens understand that you are not to be expected to put up with the ear-shattering vibrations; but since they enjoy their music so much, they'll play it loud until the last, exquisite minute and know almost precisely when you'll *make* them turn it down. But the fact is, they don't really resent it when you force them to lower the decibels. They expect it.

Get Off the Phone

Why is it such a job to pry a teenager away from your home phone or his or her cell phone? Why does it bother parents when teens spend hours talking on the phone? Most parents aren't annoyed because they're eager to make or receive a call, or reduce the phone bill. Parents have Call Waiting for that. Parents tell me it bothers them to hear their teens spend half their lives talking on the phone. They feel the teen should be doing something better with his or her time. I asked teenagers why they spend so much time on the phone, even if their parents have asked them a thousand times to give the thing a rest. They say:

▨ "The call is important, and the conversation is good. Once you get into the flow of it, you can't stop." JUDE, 15

▨ "My whole life revolves around the phone." RO, 15

▨ "Because something might have happened that I need to talk to my friends about, or maybe I'm in the middle of a fight with my boyfriend, or I'm talking to a cute guy I just met, or my friend might be telling me a juicy story." MARTHE, 16

▨ "Because I have to make important phone calls. My mother could wait a little longer." MAX, 15

■ "When you're punished and can't go out, at least you can talk over the phone, and talk your life away." LISA, 15

■ "Because I don't want to be rude to the person on the other end." CHRISTINE, 17

■ "I should have equal rights on everything." DOM, 14

■ "Because many times I've asked them to get off the phone, and they keep blabbing on, so I do it to get them back." JASMINE, 16

Teenagers stay on the phone for, first of all, the same reasons we stay on the phone: they're either talking to someone important or they're enjoying the conversation. Marthe's explanation best illustrates the fact: There could be a million reasons why they don't want to hang up. But in addition to the normal reasons that everyone stays on the phone, many teens have the misguided idea that they have, as Dom puts it, equal rights, and that they have the right to do to us what we do to them.

If your teen is under the false impression that he has equal rights, I would set him straight by reminding him who pays the bills. If that doesn't work, remove the phone from his room for one day or take away his cell phone and he'll get the message.

Many parents feel it's not worth fighting over the telephone, and they get their teens a private number, or better, for safety reasons, a cell phone. Even though this can be an expensive solution, in many ways it's more of a commonplace item than a luxury. Companies offer many phone plans today with a generous number of free hours and free long-distance calls. When the free hours are used up, the teen could be required to pay the difference from his allowance or part-time job. This method would also teach responsibility when it comes to talking on the phone and more important—paying the bill!

I Know It Was Here Yesterday—What Happened to It?

You carefully laid out your clothing the night before. You know you placed the belt to that outfit on the hanger, and behold: It's not there. You're already running late, and have not even a minute to spare looking for another belt or, worse, for another outfit. You look on the closet floor, you look on your bed. No luck. And your teen has just left for school with your belt, you are sure.

You're dressing for a party and you try to zip up your dress, but the zipper is broken. You're taking a shower and reach for your shampoo and it's gone. You're putting on your makeup, but no mascara. It's enough to make you scream, grind your teeth, or develop another furrow in your already finely etched brow.

Why can't they leave your things alone? One mother complains, "No matter how many bottles of conditioner I buy my daughter, she's sure to get my one pitiful bottle every time. It's come to the point where I actually have concealed the precious balm in an old empty peroxide bottle. But I know it's only a matter of time until she stumbles upon my secret."

I asked teenagers why they borrow their mothers' makeup, shampoo, clothing, and so forth, without asking, even though she hates that. Their answers were quite logical.

■ "Because sometimes her stuff is better than mine." MICHELLE, 15

■ "Who has the time to chase their mother around in the middle of getting ready to ask and then play twenty questions why you need it and hear that nothing better happen to it, or don't finish it, or put it right back when you're done? People know these things already." GENNA, 16

■ "Because I know she's going to say no." AVA, 13

■ "Because I'm usually having an emergency, when I'm in a mad rush to go to school or go out, or whatever." MADELINE, 16

■ "Because when I need something, I know it's there for me, even if my mother gets mad. She'll get over it." WENDY, 15

■ "She's at work when I need it." GENEVIVE, 14

■ "I love my Mom's clothes, and if I have nothing to wear, I just take her clothes. I know she hates that, but I never say anything when she wears my clothes." SANDRA, 17

■ "Because that's what daughters are for." MEG, 15

The teens are right on every count. Our stuff is better than theirs, they need something in an emergency and don't have time for a lengthy argument or a risk of no, or we are not home, so they can't ask us. We borrow their things. All true. But why don't they at least put them back?

The universal answer is: I forgot.

I thought I had the answer one day. I'll teach her a lesson, I thought. So when she wasn't home, I searched her room with glee, looking for something to hide so that she would see how it feels. I lit upon her blow-dryer, and hid it under my bed. But the plan backfired. I forgot to hide my own dryer as well, and not only did she use it, she blew it out. I thought of hiding her blusher, but then when I considered the prospect of hiding mine (and maybe forgetting where), it all seemed like so much work. I decided, forget it. I guess Meg was right: That's what daughters are for.

All kidding aside, you can keep the borrowing to a minimum by making sure your daughter is well supplied with all the necessities, or—even better—teach your teen that it's *her* responsibility to remind you well in advance if she is running out of something. Or better yet, let your teen be responsible for going to the store and buying her own shampoo or toothpaste when she runs out. You could pay for it, but she could be responsible for the legwork.

Stop Cracking That Gum

As a parent, gum snapping is, of course, the least of your problems, but many parents tell me it drives them up the wall. Why do they have to snap, crackle, and pop the gum? Teens say:

▪ "Because I like snapping my gum when it tastes so good." ZSA-ZSA, 13

▪ "It's fun to blow bubbles and pop gum." LIONEL, 15

▪ "It's a natural habit that almost everybody does." QUERESMAN, 15

▪ "When I'm really into the gum, I get carried away and I forget and start snapping it." NELLY, 17

▪ "Because I can't chew gum without snapping it." MITZI, 18

■ "Habits are hard to break. You get so used to doing it, after a while, you don't have control over it." CORDELIA, 16

■ "It's wonderful." CATHERINE, 16

■ "I get a kick out of it, and I like to bother my parents." DIONNE, 15

■ "Because they do things to me that annoy me, and they don't care, so I don't care either." RUBY, 16

■ "I think you should be able to chew the way you feel like chewing it." ETTA, 14

Most teens pop their gum for the sheer pleasure of it or out of habit, and many do it unconsciously, claiming that they can't help it. Those who admit to doing it deliberately to annoy their parents, or to get even with them for not being considerate of their dislikes, don't begin popping gum for that reason. It's already a habit, and they do it with extra pleasure at times, to annoy parents. No matter what the reason, if the habit gets on your nerves, you have a right to demand that your teen take the gum out of her mouth. End of conversation. I did it all the time. And when she would say "You're getting old, Mom. Things get on your nerves," I would quickly agree. "Yes indeed, I am. Now take it out, immediately if not sooner."

Stop Saying That

When teenagers say certain things, parents cringe. I asked teenagers what they say that drives their mother or father crazy, and what goes through their minds when their parents complain about it. Teens report the following.

▪ "When I say 'So?' or 'I don't care,' or when I huff and puff, my mother gets very irritated. I think, What does she expect me to say when she nags and criticizes me all the time?" RONALD, 17

▪ "Whenever I say, 'Oh, boy,' my parents say: I wish you would stop saying that. I think, Why are they picking on me?" MICKEY, 14

▪ "I say 'bee-bee' over and over again. I don't know why, I just feel like saying it. They keep shouting: 'Stop with the damned bee-bee,' and I think, Why does this annoy them?" MILLY, 13

▪ "She gets mad when I say, 'I'll be glad when I get older so I can live away from you.' She says: 'You're in for a big surprise.' Then I think: Will I live in peace and happiness, or loneliness?" CLAUDIA, 16

▪ "When I get disgusted and say, 'I can't take it anymore,' they say: 'Cut the dramatics. There are people with worse problems than yours.' I think, Why don't you shut up. I'll say what I feel like saying, if I feel that way. The hell with those other people. I'm not living in their shoes, and they're not living in mine. Why can't you understand that?" JENNY, 18

▪ "My parents hate when I say: 'You don't know what you're talking about.' I do it to make them unsure of their point during that particular argument, and also to annoy them. When they yell about it, sometimes I feel guilty, but then I think of what they do to cause me to talk that way, and I tell them it's their fault, and why it's their fault." JOHN, 19

▪ "My parents hate when I say, 'Leave me alone.' I do it because when they start talking about something, they never stop. Then I think, Let me go to my room before my mother smacks me." CANDIDA, 13

■ "Whenever my mother asks me a question I don't feel like answering, which is *always,* I say, 'I don't know.' This drives her mad. When she complains, I think, Aw shut up." LOTTIE, 14

■ "I say nothing, and that alone drives them crazy. I think to myself, I can't help it if I can't talk. That's my personality, that's the way I grew up, my environment, the way I am." CHRISTINE, 17

■ "My parents yell when I talk with a street accent. They say, 'Keep that talk outside.' I think, I'm sure you talked strange when you were young." JO, 13

■ "When I say: 'That sucks,' my mother says: 'Stop it or I'll wash your mouth out with soap.' I think Shut up. You talk the way you want. Give me my freedom." ANNA, 15

■ "When I say, 'damn,' my mother says it's just like saying 's—t.' I say, 'No it isn't. You always say the same thing over and over. I already know it by heart.'" ROWENA, 17

■ "When I say the f-word, my mother says: 'Melanie, do you want to get hit?' I think, 'Why can you say it, and I can't?' I know the answer, but that goes through my mind anyway. Also, I think Shut up." MEL, 16

■ "My mother hates when I have an answer for everything. I don't necessarily answer in a smart way, I just don't shut up." GAY, 14

In a certain mood, a parent does not want to hear a word or phrase repeated over and over again even if it's an innocent word like "bee-bee." Most parents hate to hear, "So what" or

"Leave me alone," and they dread hearing, "I can't take it any-more." They abhor hearing, "You don't know what you're talking about," can't abide a teen's insistence on getting the last word, and will not tolerate foul language.

When we complain about their talk, most teens would never dare to tell us exactly what's going through their minds, but as you can see, they hate our correcting their speech. They wish they were allowed to say whatever they please, and wish that we would shut up, go away, and mind our own business.

The best solution is to try to tolerate the annoying talk, and reserve putting our foot down for their cursing, vulgarity, and outright disrespect. Although teens complain when we call them out on their language, it's clear that they expect us to keep them in check if they go overboard. In fact, if we didn't, they'd feel insecure.

A Potpourri of Annoyances

What other obscure things do teens do that drive their parents crazy? And why do they continue to do those things anyway? Teens say:

▓ "I tease my younger brother. I'm bored, and it's fun to see him react." MATTHEW, 14

▓ "When I take everything as a joke, and my mother says: 'Sometimes I can kill you.' I do it because they like to make a big deal out of everything." ELLIOTT, 17

▓ "My mother hates when I bring a friend to sleep over and I don't tell her ahead of time. She says she looks forward to her privacy, and when friends sleep over, she can't totally relax. I don't see what the big deal is. Anyway, I can't plan it all the time. I like to be spontaneous." CAROL, 16

■ "When my mother says no, I beg her to change her mind. This infuriates her, but I do it because in the past, it has worked." SAMMY, 16

■ "My mother hates when I roll my eyes. She says: 'Keep it up and I'll make sure they roll to the other side of your face.' I do it when she's saying something ridiculous, and since I can't answer back, that's my only way of expressing myself." JOY, 15

■ "My mother goes wild when I walk away while she's talking. I do it when she's nagging me about something I hate to do, to get away from her voice. One time she hit me in the head with a bunch of celery she had in her hand." TODD, 16

■ "My mother hates when I make faces when she puts the dinner on the table. She says: 'Use your allowance to eat out if you don't like it.' I say: 'Why can't she make something different for a change?' and she always says the same thing: 'When you're married and you have your own family, you can cook something different 365 days of the year if you want. Until then, you'll have to eat what I put on the table.'" ELLA, 14

■ "When I suck my teeth, my mother says: 'That's one disgusting habit.' It makes me laugh when my mother gets annoyed." GLENDA, 15

■ "My father goes off when I slurp my drinks down. He says: 'The drink's not going anywhere. Take your time. You're going to be a slob when you grow up. I don't know who you take after, but it's not me.'" JOCELYN, 15

Teasing siblings, taking things lightly, inviting overnight guests without asking, refusing to take no for an answer, rolling eyes, sucking teeth, walking away while you're talking, complaining about the food, and slurping drinks may seem like relatively minor offenses, and they are but not when the heating system has broken down, your eight-year-old has the chicken pox, and your spouse is threatening to leave you.

So what do you do about these annoyances? Parents tell me they've tried everything from ignoring it until they explode, to taking away privileges, to talking until they're blue in the face, to just hoping that they themselves will survive until their teens mature.

But there is something we can do right now: talk to them. But don't just talk; communicate. Paint a clear picture for them of what it feels like to be forty and a parent. After all, we've been teenagers, and with a little work, we can at least remember how it felt for us, but they have never been our age. They have nothing to go on except for what they know as teenagers. Most teenagers are, most of the time, oblivious to the woes of a parent. They're caught up in their own world, and haven't the slightest idea how it feels to be five years on either side of forty and wanting to have some fun, too. They do not know that their parents are faced with responsibilities, responsibilities, responsibilities, instead of fun. Little do they know that we secretly dream about traveling around the world, buying a sports car, or running away from everything, but instead of realizing any of those fantasies, what we do realize is another line on our face, an extra inch of fat on our buttocks, and another gray hair.

The sad truth is (well not so sad—just Reality 101) we have rapidly approached the hill (you know, that hill we're all supposed to be going over), we will realize that someday it all ends, and we want to make a thrust for a bit of fulfillment and joy while we have some good looks and youthful energy left. But just when we have this revelation, we're unable to take action because our hands are tied. We must put ourselves aside for yet a little while longer. When teens are made to see this, they realize that it is indeed a small wonder that at times, we just can't tolerate any added frustration, and they can understand us in a way they never could before.

Why Teens Continue to Drive You Up the Wall

Even if teenagers do understand us, however, very often they continue to drive us up the wall. Why? They are just being teenagerly, so to speak. For example, when asked why, despite our pleas, they continue to do things that madden us, they say, in all honesty:

■ "I don't do it on purpose. I'm just acting like a kid or a child." PHIL, 15

■ "It's hard to remember what annoys them." DAISY, 14

■ "I don't know why. It just seems to happen." NATALIE, 16

■ "I'm my own person. This isn't Rikers Island jail you know." MARSHA, 15

■ "I guess I do it for attention." DESIREE, 14

■ "It's part of my personality." GERARD, 17

It's a little sad. Half the time, they don't even realize that they're annoying us until it's too late and we're shouting at them. They annoy us when they're just being themselves.

What can we do to remedy the situation? Here's an idea that appeals to teens' innate respect for fair play, and their desire to be treated as adults rather than babies.

Let's Make a Deal

I asked teenagers to think of one thing their parents do that annoys them, and to ask themselves if they would be willing to make a trade with them. Every teen agreed that he would stop doing one specific thing if, in return, his parents would stop doing something that annoyed him. Here are some of the proposed trades:

▨ "If she stops repeating herself, I stop ignoring her." VALERIE, 14

▨ "I would clean up my room if she would stop trying to treat me like a kid." RAYMOND, 16

▨ "I would trade her nagging for my smoking." LORALEE, 15

▨ "If she would stop telling me to go ask my father every time I want permission to do something, I would stop playing my radio loud." BLANCHE, 13

▨ "If they would stop telling me I'm still young, I would agree not to use foul language." FRANK, 17

▨ "I would stop popping gum if my father would quit making gross sounds when he eats." LISA, 13

▨ "If my father would stop teasing me and making fun of

me, I would stop rolling my eyes." JOY, 15

■ "Don't ask so many stupid questions, and I'll stop tapping my foot." RONALD, 16

■ "Quit comparing me to my older sister and I'll do my homework and get better grades." LESLIE, 16

■ "No more sweeping generalizations about my personality, such as 'You're a very . . .' or 'You'll never . . .' and I'll be more respectful in the way I talk to them." SONNY, 19

■ "Give up searching my room for things I haven't worn lately, and I'll ask every time before I borrow something." CARLA, 18

■ "Let me watch TV without interrupting, and I won't say, 'I know, I know' other times." CAMEO, 16

They want us to stop nagging? Impossible.

■ "Clean the room, pick up the shoes, wash the dishes, do your homework, and I won't have to nag." 42-YEAR-OLD FATHER

One way for teens to stop the nagging would be to simply stop what they are doing, listen to the nag, think about it, and take immediate action. Miraculously, the nagging stops. When teens try this method, they say it works. The only trouble is, half the time they don't want to stop, listen, and take action. But it's worth a try to ask your teen to try this method.

Raymond's mother could strike a bargain with him where he gets a privilege previously denied him, perhaps a later curfew or fewer questions for an agreement that on a given day each week, his room is clean and he will invite his mother in to see that he's keeping his part of the bargain. He will feel as if he's being treated less like a baby, and his mother will be happy that the room *does* get cleaned one a week.

Loralee's parents could agree to be more generous with her in a specific area if she volunteers to join a stop-smoking program. But I would suggest they take her up on her offer only if she's truly in earnest about giving up cigarettes: Breaking the habit involves real commitment, not just a vague gesture.

Blanche's parents can take advantage of an opportunity for the wife to stop passing the buck to the husband whenever Blanche asks for a decision or a favor; it's something they should do together anyway, whether or not in exchange for a little more peace and quiet.

Frank's parents can agree to stop using the expression, "You're still young" in exchange for his agreement to cut down on the cursing: In fact it's a perfect deal, because as I'm sure they have already pointed out, when you're a kid cursing is offensive but understandable. When you're a man, it's uncouth and a sign of immaturity.

Chances are, Lisa's father has no idea that he's making loud noises when he eats, noises that can be just as annoying, if not more so, than Lisa's gum popping. If she told him how it gets on her nerves, he would be able to relate to it by thinking of how he feels when she pops her gum, and chances are, he would agree to work on it.

Joy hates her father's teasing, Ronald hates stupid questions, Leslie abhors being compared, Sonny dislikes being put down, Carla hates having her room searched, and Cameo dislikes being interrupted. What do you do that bothers your teenager? Since you probably already have a mental list of things your teen does that annoy you, pick something and see if your teen is willing to make a trade. You can say something like, "Let's exchange lists. You write a list of things I do that drive you crazy, and I will write a list of things you do that drive me crazy. Then we'll see if we can both agree on an even exchange: I stop doing something that bothers you, and you stop doing something that bothers me." You'll probably be surprised by how well this simple bargain works. You will almost certainly be surprised to read the following sequence of words: Teens are usually even better than parents at keeping their part of the bargain.

Still, there's no easy solution. Teenagers, by their very nature, will drive you slightly mad. Understanding them helps a lot; little tricks help a little.

Reminders

1. Loud music is to teenagers as shrieking is to toddlers. It's an outlet they love because it is an expression of their joy of living. It also relaxes and soothes them.
2. Teenagers realize they will be asked to turn the music down. However, they love it so much, they wait until they are asked a second time, a third. . . .
3. Teenagers feel that the phone is their lifeline to the social scene, and many of them mistakenly believe that they have equal rights with parents to the phone. Either make

firm telephone rules or get your teen his own number and or cell phone, and work out an agreement about paying the bill.

4. Teenagers borrow their parents' toiletries, clothing, and other articles because it's convenient to do so, the quality is better, and they know they can get away with their depredations. Keep them supplied with the necessities, but realize that to a teen, *your* stuff will always seem better.

5. If your teenager's language annoys you, save putting your foot down for the really unacceptable.

6. To help your teen understand why you are grouchy or critical, paint a clear picture for him of what it feels like to be fortyish and a parent with a whole lot of responsibilities.

7. Make a deal with your teen. Agree to stop doing one thing that annoys her if she will stop doing one thing that annoys you.

8. Understand that teenagers will always annoy parents. The idea is to cling to your sanity and realize that this, too, shall pass.

Chapter 7

You're Not Leaving This House Dressed That Way

How many times have you had arguments with your teenager because of his or her dress, hairstyle, or makeup?

■ "She says her hairstyle is in, but to me it looks like a cock's tail." 36-YEAR-OLD MOTHER

■ "What is he thinking about? Bleached jeans with a huge tear right in the butt area? I've raised a bum." 45-YEAR-OLD MOTHER

■ "He's dressed for August in the dead of winter. God give me strength for this child." 47-YEAR-OLD FATHER

■ "She looks like a walking sex advertisement." 43-YEAR-OLD MOTHER

Why do teenagers want to appear outrageous? Is it just a stage they will grow out of? Should we leave them alone until they do? Should we let them *dye their hair purple and wear rags to school if they please?* We have to draw the line somewhere, don't we?

Who Taught You to Dress?

Teenagers complain about parents' reactions to their ways of dressing.

■ "My mother has a heart attack when I wear this satin miniskirt. I tell her this is the style!" MIRIAM, 16

■ "I wear sweats to school and my dad says I'm not dressed properly. People don't dress formal anymore. Why can't he wake up?" CARL, 16

■ "When I wear net stockings, my mother says I look cheap. Why doesn't she look at her old photo albums?" MARITZA, 14

■ "I was going to a club, and my mother was away in Florida at the time, and my father and I always argue whenever she isn't there. I had on this skimpy tank top, but I had a long dress-coat over it that wasn't going to come off anyway. He told me I looked trampy. If I would have taken the coat off, it would have been trampy, but I wasn't going to, so what was the big deal?" JENNIFER, 16

■ "My mother yells at me when I wear a T-shirt without a bra." GEE-GEE, 15

■ "When I wear red lipstick, they say I look like a clown. We have major fights over my lipstick." KATY, 13

■ "I was wearing green eye shadow and other makeup, and my mother wouldn't let me go to the dance until I scrubbed it off. I was so furious. I was crying and everything. Of course, I put it on at my girlfriend's house anyway." EVANGELINE, 15

■ "When I just throw anything on and don't match, my mother says: 'Take that off. You look like terrible.'" SANDRA, 16

■ "When I wear my cap backward, my parents reprimand me." MONY, 15

■ "When will my father learn that no one ties sneakers these days?" NAT, 17

▧ "When I dress like a heavy-metal rock star in leather pants and jacket, and wear bandannas all over, they tell me I look like a punk, and that's not the way they want me to dress." MICHAEL, 15

If your teen wears ripped, faded, mismatched, old, or otherwise odd-looking clothing, what harm is there? Who is Mony hurting if he wears his cap backward? Why not let Nat wear his laces the way he wants to? After all, if he trips on them, he'll learn for himself. Face it, he's too old for his father to protect anyway. Does the backward cap indicate rebellion or disrespect? To you it may symbolize just that, but to a teen, all it usually means is "I'm cool." And if teens need anything, it's to feel cool. Of course, he'll soon not need the outward symbol, because he will have finished the work of growing up, and his maturity, we may hope, will allow him to find signals of coolness coming from within him. But in the meantime why not agree to let him dress the way he wants to for school and for when he's with his friends, and ask him to agree to modify his attire for you, on special occasions such as weddings, bar mitzvahs, and other more formal situations.

It may bother you to see your teen dressed like everybody else. But to a teen, dressing like other teens in his or her crowd *is* dressing uniquely, because it is at least different from the way the older generation dresses. (That's one reason, by the way, teens feel uncomfortable when parents try to dress too much like teenagers.)

But what about revealing clothing or seemingly suggestive makeup? With popular young talents like Britney Spears and others, even preteens have taken up an extremely seductive look. We have to face it: These young rising stars are the new role models for our teens.

Should a 13-year-old be allowed to wear red lipstick, then? Maybe not. But rather than forbid it, I would keep telling her how much prettier she looks in the lighter shades. If it really bothers you, however, you can put your foot down and refuse to let her leave the house as Britney. However, try not to become overly upset if you find out that she's been putting it on once she gets to school and taking it off before she gets home. It's normal teenage behavior and not something I would make a life-and-death issue. Most teens, like Evangeline, who puts her green eye shadow on at her friend's house, will find a way to paint their faces the way they see fit until they grow out of that stage. Parents who forbid the makeup should be content to know that at least they are spared the unpleasant sight. Why play detective and inflict major punishments for such little rebellions? Teens, in fact, need to think they're getting away with *something.*

The best thing you can do now is to continually stress good taste, and to mention that you know your teen will eventually develop a sense of what is most flattering. For example, one mother told me that when her daughter wears a too-tight, too-short skirt, she tells her daughter that if she's trying to look appealing to boys, she's not achieving her goal. Guys don't really like that look on a girl. They prefer a more subdued, sensuous look, not a blatantly sexy look. In fact, often they perceive the come-on look as threatening. The mother told me that her daughter insists that she doesn't know what she's talking about, but tends not to wear the disputed outfit very often after that.

Each parent has a different level of tolerance when it comes to seductive clothing. You have a right to refuse to let your teen wear something you find highly offensive. However, try to tolerate as much as you can. For example, net stockings may look cheap to most parents, but if they're the style, it's better to save "You're not leaving this house dressed that way" for the see-through blouse or skimpy tank top. The fact is, if you come down hard on your teen about everything he or she wears, you'll alienate your teen. You've really got to let things go when you can, so your word will carry more weight when your message really matters. If you protest everything, your teen will end up thinking you're really out of it, and that you don't know what you're talking about. (Most teens claim their parents don't know the first thing about clothes and makeup, but in their heart of hearts, they know their parents are often right, especially when it comes to how far to go with suggestive clothing.)

That Hairstyle Has Got to Go

Similarly, it's appalling when our teenagers sabotage their good looks with unflattering hairstyles. We hate to see that the little doll whose hair we used to comb exactly to our liking now looks like something out of a horror flick. Teens talk about how parents feel about their lovely coiffures:

▧ "My mother says I look like a bird that tried to struggle out of a cage. What makes her think her hair looks any better?"
LEILA, 14

■ "She says: 'Your hair is plastered to your head.' What does she know? That's the style." DANIELLE, 15

■ "My father told me I look like I put my finger in a socket. I'm the one wearing it. I like it that way." YVONNE, 17

■ "My mother said my braids look tacky. Too bad. I like them." JUDY, 15

■ "My father said my hairstyle made me look slutty and hard looking. I was very hurt by his remarks." GINGER, 15

■ "I like wearing long hair, and all I ever hear is 'You look like a girl.' That's so stupid. Everyone knows that these days there's no set style. Anything goes. And why does it bother them so much, anyway? Can't they let me do anything without making a big deal of it?" RENO, 16

Do Teenagers Learn to Correct Their Own Appearance?

Listen to this:

■ "When I was 13 and 14, I used to wear my hair so far out on the sides, it looked like I had elephant ears. I never did the back of my hair either, so it was totally flat. I looked stupid. I would never wear it that way now because I realize how horrible it looked and I can see it in old pictures. I look much better now. It took me almost two years to see that." WILLOW, 16

■ "I used to be into heavy metal and I dressed for that style. Now I'm following a more neutral style." DICK, 17

■ "My sister wears her hair all teased out the way I used to wear it two years ago. I see now that it did look ridiculous, but she won't listen to me when I tell her either." TOOTSIE, 16

▨ "When I was 13, my hair stood straight up, and people used to stare. My parents would insult me, and I would hate them for it. Now that I'm mature, I would never be seen in public that way." BERYL, 17

▨ "I had shaved the sides of my head and dyed the rest purple and pink. I looked like a fool." SUE-ANN, 18

▨ "Last year my hair was really short, and the top went back, and I wore it with a few bangs down. It looked like a cobra. I would never wear my hair that way again." ERIKA, 15

▨ "Looking back, I could see how childish I was then. The style didn't go with my face and it was unflattering." BETSY, 16

At What Age Should You Step Aside?

At what age should a child, preteen, or teen dress or wear his or her hair the way he or she chooses? Teenagers have very definite opinions on when the right time is, and can back them up with reasons:

▨ "At seven or eight, because they need to learn responsibility." JANNETTE, 16

▨ "At nine, because they should learn to have enough sense to know what to wear." KENT, 17

▨ "At 10. That's when my body started to change and I looked silly in certain clothes." DAISY, 14

▨ "At 11, because by then a child would have developed a taste of his own." ROSS, 15

■ "At 12, because it would get them ready for being a teenager." MARSHA, 15

■ "At 13, because that's when children need to wear what everyone else is wearing." LINA, 15

■ "At 14, because by then if you look stupid, you'll find it out on your own and you need to learn things on your own." FRIEDA, 16

■ "At 15. After that it becomes annoying to be told." JACK, 15

■ "Never. Children always need advice from their parents. If someone looks ridiculous, it's better that their parents tell them, to save them further embarrassment." MARYLYN, 15

It's a good idea to start letting your child select from two or three outfits starting as early as age five or six. By 10 or 11, you can let your child choose color and style with a little advice from you when you take him or her clothing shopping. By 14 or 15, a teen should be allowed to make his or her own choices within the limit of your budget, of course. Naturally you will express your opinion, but take care to avoid such comments as "You have bad taste," and "You must be blind." Teens need to develop their own style, and they feel crushed when a parent insults their choices. Negative comments destroy self-esteem. It's much better to say things like "You and I have such different tastes in clothing. I would have chosen the royal blue."

Would Teens Put Restrictions on Their Own Teens' Dress and Hairstyles?

Of course they would.

▪ "I wouldn't let them wear clothes that were too revealing or made them look like a slob." BILL, 17

▪ "I would let her wear anything she wants, as long as it's conservative." DONNETTE, 16

▪ "Yes and no. I wouldn't be strict with what they wore or they would just rebel. I know it's just a stage that they go through, so as long as there was a certain amount of decency." GINNY, 16

▪ "Yes. I would make a restriction that they not wear tight pants or short skirts." LESLIE, 16

▪ "I would not let my daughter wear miniskirts or tight-fitting tops." FLORA, 14

▪ "My son or daughter will not go out looking like a whore or a pimp, and they will not look homeless." TOM, 17

Evidently these teens are absorbing some of the standards of their parents after all. Amazing, isn't it?

What Did You Look Like When You Were a Teenager?

If you're still not comforted, perhaps a little trip down memory lane is in order. I asked parents to describe their own dress or hairstyle when they were teens, a look that their own parents complained about.

■ "I teased my hair into a balloonlike bouffant." 42-YEAR-OLD MOTHER

■ "My beehive could *really* nest bees." 46-YEAR-OLD MOTHER

■ "My hair was very, very long. I looked like the wolfman." 36-YEAR-OLD FATHER

■ "I wore the DA, better know as the duck's ass. I looked like a guy." 47-YEAR-OLD MOTHER

■ "I had long, straight, stringy, dirty hair." 38-YEAR-OLD MOTHER

■ "I wore a leather jacket, motorcycle boots, and studded garrison belt, and so did every guy in my group of friends." 52-YEAR-OLD FATHER

■ "Ha. I wore an Afro, a dashiki, and lots of beads. I even changed my name to Abdul something or other. Now I'm a conservative Wall Street broker." 57-YEAR-OLD FATHER

■ "I wore a mini that just about covered my you-know-what, and platform heels." 35-YEAR-OLD MOTHER

If you don't believe it, pull out the old albums. Those teenagers who looked at old photos of their parents reported that they were shocked to see some of the outlandish styles: bell-bottoms, tight hip-huggers, high boots, hippy-type dress, no bra, really *big* eighties hair, lots of glitter and silver lamé, and on and on. Can you identify yourself in any of these styles?

I asked teenagers, "If you could teach parents a lesson about the way teenagers dress and wear their hair, what lesson would that be?" They say the following.

▪ "Soon it will be over. It's just a phase. Let us go through it." DREW, 14

▪ "Teenagers are just learning what life is all about. Let us learn some lessons for ourselves." JOHNNY, 18

▪ "We're not out to be rebellious. We just want to have a good time." CAROLYN, 13

▪ "Teenagers are going to wear what they think is in style. Period." ELVIS, 19

▪ "They should learn to cope with us!" FRANK, 15

▪ "They were teens, too, and they wore cockroach shoes so let us be teens and wear whatever." CRAIG, 16

▪ "Leave us alone and it will be that much sooner we realize how ridiculous we look." JENNIFER, 16

▪ "Stop pestering us to look like a nerd." RO, 15

▪ "Let them know how they look, but don't heavily criticize or totally forbid them. They just hate you and rebel more." EILEEN, 17

▪ "Don't compare the styles of today with those of the past." EDGAR, 14

Enough said!

Reminders

1. Make a deal with your teenager. Within the limits of decency, he dresses the way he wants when he's with his friends and when he goes to school, but he will modify his dress for you on special occasions.
2. To a teen, dressing like everybody else means dressing

differently, because it's not the way adults dress.

3. If you think your teenager looks hideous because of dress, hairstyle, or makeup, realize that teens themselves correct themselves even in later teenage stages. If you doubt that your teenager will eventually become civilized, look at your old photo albums. How did you look as a teenager?

4. If your teenager sneaks behind your back to wear forbidden makeup, don't make a federal case out of it. Sometimes it's better to overlook the small things. Teenagers do need to rebel a little. Save coming down hard on them for the big things.

5. If you can't let your teen wear her choice of clothing because it's indecent, try to allow her the hairstyle (even if it offends your taste).

6. It's a good idea to let your teenager select his own clothing, within the limits of your budget. If your teen's taste clashes with yours, try to express your opinion without insulting him.

7. If you want to find out if your teen is absorbing some of your ideas about dress and hairstyles, ask her what restrictions she would put on her teenager's dress, hairstyle, and makeup if she were a parent.

8. What may seem like rebellious styles to a parent—cap worn to the side or spiked hair—is usually only a teenager's way of saying "I'm cool."

Chapter 8
Talk to Me

Wouldn't it be wonderful if, when your teenager had a problem, you were the first one he or she came to for help? Teenagers feel insecure, guilty, angry, depressed, confused, scared, and often helpless. Yet most often, and most unfortunately, the last ones they turn to for help are their parents. A parent complains:

■ "If I ask what's wrong, I can put money on getting the same answer: 'Nothing, Ma. Leave me alone.' What can I do to get her to talk?" 41-YEAR-OLD MOTHER

In this chapter, you'll discover exactly why teens don't come to you first, and better yet, you'll learn how to change the situation—it won't be as difficult as you think. It will, however, involve breaking a habit, biting your tongue, and biding your time. More on that later.

Why Teenagers Don't Talk to Their Parents

Most teenagers would love to confide in their parents and have tried to, many times. But the moment they start relating their experience, they're interrupted by a parent who launches a lecture on the subject or reprimands them. Are you guilty of what these teens say their parents do?

■ "I was happy that this boy paid for my lunch, so I told my father, and before I could even finish, he said he didn't want me to accept anything from boys because they might want something in return. When he said that, it was as if he held up a big sign stating I Don't Understand Anything. All boys are not the same. But I just said 'Okay, Dad,' and made up my mind to keep my big mouth shut next time." PATTY, 15

■ "I got kicked out of driver's ed class, and I was upset about it, so I told my mother what happened. Before I could explain the details, she said: 'You're in the wrong. You shouldn't have cut off those old people.' I wanted to get to the part where the teacher had distracted me, but she didn't give me a chance. All she did was accuse me, so I said to myself 'What a waste,' and walked away mad." PAUL, 18

■ "I told my mother about a joke we played on a friend, and immediately she said it's wrong to do that. I stopped talking, because I thought she would really get on my case if I told her the really bad part." BARBARA, 16

■ "I had told my father that this girl wanted to have sex with me, but I turned her down because she was pushy, and immediately he started to lecture me about AIDS, which had nothing to do with what I was saying. I realized I was stupid to expose myself that way, and I made up my mind not to make that mistake again." ERROL, 16

■ "One day I was upset because of a fight I had, and I was telling my mother about it, but before I could finish, she started saying that girls don't look right fighting—that's for animals. Because she got so excited and highly activated, and started talking away, I said to myself, 'Oh boy, I wish I never told her.'" JULIA, 14

▨ "I told my mom about my boyfriend, and my mom starts saying 'You're too young to be getting yourself in trouble, and he's four years older than you,' and on and on. I didn't finish, because no one cared. What a hypocrite she is. First she says 'Talk to me,' then when I do, she condemns me." SABRINA, 14

▨ "I came home very late one night because my date's car broke down, and we had to push it to a gas station. I was upset because I knew my mother would worry. I never got a chance to explain, because she went crazy when I came in. I ended up crying in my room and throwing things around. What frustrated me the most was she wouldn't be quiet for a minute so I could explain what happened." GLENDA, 17

▨ "I was trying to explain to my father that I was kidding with my mother when I spoke to her in a certain way. He wouldn't listen. He just screamed. I was so mad that he cut me off and started lecturing. I didn't feel he was even worthy of hearing the rest. I didn't want to waste my breath on him." JAY, 19

▨ "On the way home from school, I stopped off at the store with my friend, and this man was holding up the store so when I came home, I was shook up, and I wanted to tell my mother what happened, but when I started, she cut me off and said: 'I told you to come straight home and not stop anywhere. Next time you'll be punished.' Because of what she said, I decided not to tell her the ending as it happened, and I wished I never told her." ROCHELLE, 15

▨ "I started telling my father how I almost got in trouble hanging out with this friend. Before I could explain, I got a lecture. I didn't finish, because I got upset when he started jumping to conclusions without letting me explain." JOHN, 17

■ "I told my father that I had an argument with a man on the train, and he said: 'That man could have shot your brains out,' and he went on and on. He didn't give me a chance to tell him what happened. I wished I never mentioned it." TERRY, 15

■ "We were watching this movie, and the daughter in the movie was yelling at her mother. I was getting ready to say that the girl was wrong for yelling at her mother, but my mother thought I was going to defend the girl, so before I could get my point across, she said: 'Don't you ever think about yelling at me like that. Understand?' What a pain!" SHARELL, 16

■ "I told my mother I lost my gold nameplate, and immediately she said: 'You're so careless. I told you not to wear it to school. You're not getting another one.' I was so-o-o-o sorry I told her. I said to myself, I should have made up a story." GAIL, 13

■ "I was telling my mother about a fight I had in hockey, and immediately she said: 'See? I told you hockey is too rough.' I get so sick of her because she never stops repeating herself." JARED, 18

The most difficult thing in the world is to sit there and listen to your teenager tell you that he did something that you think is wrong or harmful, and say nothing pejorative. But if you don't use restraint, you can rest assured your teen will clamp up and, as you've just read, resolve never again to make the mistake of letting you in on his or her world.

What, then, should you do if your teen tells you a story and you want to reprimand immediately? *Bite your tongue. Say nothing.* Be sympathetic. Give moral support to your child. Make supportive comments. For example, Rochelle's mother could have said: "You must have been scared to death when the man was holding up the store," and Paul's mother could have said something like: "There are two sides to a story. I'll bet your driver's ed teacher wasn't being fair." Certainly Errol's father should have said something like: "I would have felt the same way you did. It would really turn me off if a girl was that aggressive," instead of missing the point and seizing the opportunity to talk instead about AIDS, not that this conversation should not take place. It should. More about that later.

One night when Marthe was 16, I picked her up at a girl-friend's house, and she seemed very upset, so I asked her what was wrong. "Nothing," she said. But I could tell she wanted to talk, so I said, "Whatever it is, I'm sorry for you. You look hurt." With that she spilled out a story that went something like this: "There were lots of kids over, and Tom and I were in Lisa's room, just talking, but when we came out, Lisa said that Tom and I were on her bed, and she said she didn't want me in her house anymore and she embarrassed me in front of everyone."

You can imagine the things that went through my mind all at once. I wanted to blurt out: "Well, were you on the bed? What were you doing in the room with a boy with the door closed? You know I don't allow that. Where was Lisa's mother? I thought you said she would be home. I thought I could trust you." But I bit my tongue and said none of it, because the crestfallen look on my daughter's face told me that what she needed right now was comfort and moral support, not reprimands, pointed inquiries, and lectures, and that if I was suspicious or judgmental now, she would not only clam up, but resolve never again to trust me with something so sensitive and personal.

I instead said: "Lisa had some nerve insulting you that way. I wonder what made her do it. I thought she was your friend." My comment triggered a storm of anger against Lisa: "Just because Lisa does things," Marthe said, "doesn't mean she has to accuse me of doing them." She then told me that she was especially hurt because she and Tom were just getting to know each other, and were only talking, laughing, and joking in the room; Lisa had made something more of it. I continued to be tempted to ask her if anything did go on, or to lecture her about the perils of being behind closed doors with a boy, but I didn't (even though I secretly thought she probably was doing a lot more than talking). Yet again, I knew that she needed comfort, and no matter what she was or wasn't doing, her friend had been cruel to her.

Calm now, she reached out and hugged me and said: "I love you, Mommy. I don't know what I would do without you," and she went to bed. The next day she called Lisa, and somehow they straightened the whole thing out.

Later, she showed me a note Lisa had written, apologizing for what she had done. After listening, and agreeing with her about how great it was that the situation had been resolved, I said, "Marthe, where was Lisa's mother on Friday night? I thought you said she would be home." She said, "Oh, she went out, but Lisa's older sister was there. She's 19." Then I gave my lecture, reminding her that we had agreed she was not to be in homes with teens unsupervised. I also took the opportunity to talk about my feelings about her being alone in bedrooms with boys and the emotional and physical perils of teenage sexual activity. She listened to me with full attention, making comments and reassuring me that she would take my words to heart.

"So what," you might be saying, "she will still do the same thing next time." Maybe. But had I started reprimanding and accusing the moment she told her story, not only would she do the same thing next time, she also would have had to bear her humiliation and self-doubt alone. She would have felt even more betrayed and alienated when, after Lisa's attack, I attacked her. She would have shut out my words the moment I began to lecture, and gone away angry and hidden from me behind the closed door of her room. At least this way she heard me out, really listening. As a result, my words, having registered with my daughter, would stand the next time they were needed, to help keep her from making a mistake. Let's face it—if they don't hear you in the first place, they can't remember. (And that they do remember and sometimes even heed what they've heard is proven in Chapter 10.)

Let me give you another example from my experience with Marthe. One day she came home from school angry with her best friend, Jennifer. She told me that a boy was driving them home from school, and began driving wildly. "Jennifer started screaming, 'Let me out of the car,'" she said. As soon as I heard this, I was tempted to say: "I thought I told you not to go in cars with teenage drivers. You could get killed." But I kept my cool. She went on: "I think Jennifer acts like an old lady. Do you think I was right or she was right? She got mad because I didn't agree with her, and I was laughing the whole time." I was tempted to take Jennifer's part, which, of course, would have been a disaster, a guaranteed way to get Marthe to cut me out. So I said, "If it were me, I would have been scared. No one thinks they will ever die, but every day thousands of people get killed in car accidents." Then I started laughing, and asked: "Marthe, what would you have done if as soon as you told me about the boy driving wildly, I had said: 'You shouldn't have been in the car, it's dangerous, et cetera?'" She said: "I thought of that, and I was tempted to change the story a little. But I figured I'd take a chance. I'm glad you didn't say that, because I wouldn't have finished the story. I'm still trying to figure out my morals, and that's why I tell you things." I thought, "Isn't that something!"

At first I couldn't see what great moral issue was involved. But then I realized that to teens, who are just putting everything together, an issue such as how much loyalty we owe our friends when we disagree with them is major. When teens tell their parents about an event, it's because they're asking for a mirror in which to reflect their thoughts. If we listen without immediately judging, or give our opinion by telling how we would have felt rather than telling them how *they should feel,* we give them a chance to develop their character and their philosophy of life.

Think of your own teenager. I'll bet you can think of a time when he or she started telling you something and you interrupted with a reprimand or a warning. And I'll bet your teen stopped talking, or the two of you got into an argument.

Even if you have a whole history of such mistakes, all is not lost. Fortunately, teenagers are more resilient than adults. Even though they may say they will never tell you anything again—and they mean it at the time, and maybe next time, still smarting, they'll withhold the story—ultimately, they *will* again confide in you, or try to. Teens can't help but reach out. It's part of the nature of being a teenager. Bide your time, and *next* time do it right.

Teenagers want to talk to their parents. In fact, they're dying because they can't. Most teens who commit suicide are those who feel they can't talk to either parent. Their feelings of loneliness and alienation bring about the ultimate despair.

I Wish I Could Talk to My Parents About . . .

Teenagers lament:

■ "I could never talk to my father about my future, because the minute I start, he begins to tell, not ask or suggest, what I should be: something that is financially stable like a doctor, a lawyer, or a computer programmer. When I tell him I might want to become a professional dancer, he has a fit. I'm in a special dance program now for five years, and when I finally got him to go to a recital, I got a standing ovation. But after it was over, the first thing he said to me was: 'I don't like you dancing. It's a waste of time and money.' From then on, I never talked to him about my future." LISANDRA, 17

■ "I wish I could talk to my parents about drugs, but they can't deal with it. The minute I start, they lecture and condemn me, or tell me not to talk like that. So what happens is, I talk to my friends and I'm more tempted to experiment. They're totally close-minded. If they would talk to me as things come up, maybe they could share their wisdom and satisfy my curiosity, and throw in some advice here and there." VINNIE, 18

▨ "I wish I could talk to my mother about my being in love. When I try to bring up the subject, she says, 'You're so young. You have no idea what love is. You don't know what you want at this age.' I feel that she just doesn't understand that I have real feelings." CATHERINE, 15

▨ "I want to talk to my mother about my boyfriend, but my mother can't stand him, so when I bring him up, she says: 'I don't want to hear about it.' It feels lonely to have to keep everything to myself, but I have no choice." RONNIE, 14

▨ "I can't talk to my mother about dates with girls because she always makes negative comments about them. So I talk to my father." JED, 18

▨ "I wish I could talk to my parents about my older brother, who was on drugs and is living away from home now. Whenever I bring him up, they say he's past and forgotten. They don't care if he's dead. I feel so sorry for him, and I wish I could find him and help him, but if I ask about him, they change the subject. I think they're ashamed and feel sorry for him, but they just don't want to admit it." SHERON, 16

▨ "I wish I could talk to my parents about money. Whenever I try, we get into a hassle about why don't I get a job. I'm only 15 and don't have to work, keep up my grades, and still play a sport, never mind a social life." RICHARD, 15

Evidently, Lisandra's father can't cope with the idea of her becoming something so frivolous as a dancer, so he refuses to acknowledge that his daughter has a talent and a mind of her own. Doesn't he realize that all he accomplishes by throwing a wet blanket on her dream is to shut her out? A more productive idea would be to listen to her ideas for the future, compliment her wonderful performance, and then say something like: "On the other hand, have you considered . . . ?" Then he could bring home pamphlets, college brochures, and other materials outlining the careers he thinks she would also be talented in. But he should stress the element of talent and not bone-dry practicality. Most teenagers, especially creative ones, are not very impressed with arguments that emphasize only security and ignore the individuality and talent.

Vinnie is evidently willing to share his temptations, doubts, and fears regarding drugs. His parents are missing out on a golden opportunity to help him when they lecture and condemn before they hear what he has to say. Before a parent speaks, he or she must stop and think of the goal: If it is to understand and then help the teen, then the parent must first listen to statements that may grate on the parent's nerves such as discussing cocaine or ecstasy. It is not harmful to realize that teenagers often make such statements, not because they are convinced of their truth, but because they are asking to be set straight. Teens fear that the opposite of pro-drug assertions are the truth, and are begging their parents to convince them in order to help them to gain the willpower to do what is right.

The best way to handle a conversation on drugs is to listen, and then ask questions. Later you can give examples from things you've read or people you've known, and state the hard facts that are now documented regarding the harmful effects of drugs. (If you don't know them, do your homework. The bookstores are filled with factual books on the detrimental effects of drugs.) Then ask your teen what he or she thinks of it. Never argue. It's neither necessary nor helpful. In fact, an argument on whether or not drugs are damaging is equivalent to engaging in a dispute on whether or not the world is round. Vinnie's parents probably allow his provocative comments to set them off, and perhaps they panic at the thought of his possibly being involved in drugs, and begin shouting questions such as: "Are you doing drugs? Is that what this is all about?"

Catherine and Ronnie want to talk to their parents about boys, but because their parents aren't ready to accept the fact that their daughters have reached this stage of development, they brush them off. What they fail to see is that the girls are feeling insecure because of the new-felt emotions, and are reaching out to their parents for reassurance. By shutting them out with statements like "I don't want to hear it," or undermining their feelings by saying "You're too young to know," they throw away the opportunity to help their daughters to build self-confidence in the area of love and romance. What they need to hear from parents is that their budding emotions are normal and will recur many times in their lives and that their feelings are *most* intense during the teen years *because* they are new.

It sounds to me as if Jed's mother is jealous that her son is seeing girls at all, and can't cope with the idea of her son growing up and leaving the nest. Wise Jed perceives that he risks a tirade of insults against his current flame but, luckily for him, he can talk to his father. His mother gives up the opportunity to have a significant influence on his choice of girlfriends because of her condemning attitude. If she could restrict her comments to questions such as "Do you have fun when you're out together?" or "What do you two talk about?" or "What do you like best about her, and what do you think is her greatest fault?" Jed would end up revealing her faults himself, and then his mother could compliment him on his insight.

Instead of taking a hard stance and denying their grief, Sheron's parents would be better off sharing their sorrow with Sheron. She perceives their disappointment and pain anyway, but because of her parents' attitude, she is unable to talk with them. This causes her stress and perhaps even guilt because she's unable to help her brother or even to talk about him. She's taught to be ashamed of him. Also, she must be terrified. "If I make one mistake, maybe they'll banish me, too."

With our children, honesty is definitely the best policy. It is better to tell them how we really feel and why than to suppress our emotions or devise elaborate coverups. Mental health can never flourish under a pack of lies. Teenagers, let's remember, are as intelligent now as they will ever be. They may not be as mature as they will become, but that's why we have to be honest with them so they can develop their maturity, which comes only with life's real problems and sorrows. By sharing our own troubles with our teens, we give them an opportunity to grow and understand us better, and to realize that whatever is troubling us is not necessarily their fault. Too many teens end up in a therapist's office years later trying to uncover the basis of their own feelings of guilt. When you share your sorrows with your teen, there's a bonus in it for you, too. You gain comfort from them and you feel closer to your teenager. Love grows.

Learning to listen is another skill that parents need to work on. Richard's plight is a good example. He's under a lot of pressure, and he's practically crying out for help, yet his father can think of nothing more to say than "Get a job." If his parents listened to him, they might help him to better organize his time, or they might realize that at this point it's not in his best interest to have a job. Maybe a compromise could be worked out by which he works in the summer but devotes the school year to his many activities. After all, he is only 15.

Ever Try to Talk to Your Parents about Sex?

I've saved the hottest topic for last. Why do teens feel they can't talk to their parents about sex? Here's what they say:

■ "I can't talk to my mother about what I know about sex, because she feels a girl my age shouldn't know about these things. If I bring it up, she always manages to change the subject." EDWINA, 16

■ "I'm afraid my parents would be disappointed in me if I told them the truth about my sexual experiences." SALLY, 16

■ "Sex is a closed book in my house. I feel my mother has some skeletons in her closet. The only way I'll get it out of her is when she's old and senile, and talks about all the devious things she did." MARY, 15

■ "My mother never gave me the feeling that I could trust her. I remember how she jumped down my sister's throat when she had some problems with sex." VERONICA, 17

▨ "I'm afraid they might say 'Who did you have sex with?' even though I never had sex." PENNY, 13

▨ "I don't feel comfortable about it. I guess I respect them too much. Anyway, I know almost everything already. I learned it in sex education in school, which I think is very important. I also experienced having sex, too." ALEX, 16

▨ "I tried to talk to my father about sex, but he didn't want to listen to me. I guess he's scared of his little girl getting hurt, because any time the topic comes up, he cuts me off and won't let me finish. And he gets an attitude." PEPPER, 17

Apparently, most teenagers fear that if they express themselves openly to their parents about sex, they would end up being condemned or judged and, unfortunately, some of them are correct. Sex is and always has been a hot topic. I grew up with certain sexual standards, and I found it hard to accept that teenagers, even young teenagers, are sexually active. How, then, could my daughter talk openly to me about sex? Well, she didn't talk about herself. Wisely, she talked about her friends. And when I answered, I took into account that my daughter might be applying my advice and my opinion to herself. Our mode of communication may not have been ideal, but a side angle is better than no angle at all.

If you want your teenager to talk to you about sex, the best thing is to refrain from lecturing until you hear the whole story. Then, when you feel you must lecture, bring into your talk information about the way you were brought up, and how you feel about sex. You can then talk about friends you've known, or even experiences you've had that made you feel the way you do. You can tell your teen how you wish she would conduct herself sexually, and why.

For example, you might talk about a friend of yours who has been sexually active, and has contracted a variety of sexually transmitted diseases (STDs) and may be unable to bear children because of it. You could explain how although most people know that AIDS kills, they are not aware of how many other STDs are out there, and although they don't result in death, they do have dire consequences—inability to bear children being one of them.

Talk calmly. Respect your teen's intelligence. Remember, as tempting as it may be, if you threaten, judge, or condemn your teen, you'll surely drive him or her into a total secrecy and perhaps even into promiscuity by way of rebellion against you.

Think of this. If you tell your daughter "If you ever come home pregnant, I'll kill you!" what do you think will happen if she gets pregnant? You'll be the last to know. She will go through a secret abortion, as did two (at least) of my daughter's friends. Can you imagine how lonely and scary it must be for a teenager to have to bear that burden alone? If we put too much fear upon them, they may even come to see suicide as a welcome alternative.

If you feel uncomfortable about talking about sex, admit to your teen that you get embarrassed talking about it, but you'd like to try anyway. If your parents never talked about sex with you, tell them that, too. You can ask them questions about how teens in their school feel about sex, and so on. By asking your teen to educate you, you show that you don't see yourself as judge and critic.

I asked teenagers, "In your opinion, how many 16-year-old girls have already had sex? I'm told that at least 50 percent have, and I can't believe it." Then they told me, "You have no idea what it is out there. Even *more* than 50 percent."

I deliver my speeches about waiting to have sex, or at least using protection if they insist upon having sex. I tell them how nobody believes they will get AIDS, herpes, or any other STD, but every year more and more teens are contracting these diseases and sadly are also dying from them. The teens listen to me *because I have listened to them.*

Think of it this way: It's easy to talk about sex to a teen who wants to talk about it. You're lucky if your teen does. So if you're embarrassed when asking questions about other teens and talking about your upbringing, there's a reward for you: Y ou've already opened the door to communicate effectively about sex.

Advice from Teens: If You Really Want Me to Confide in You . . .

When parents ask their teenagers "What's wrong?" or "How was school?" or "Did you have a good time at the dance?" they can be guaranteed one-word answers like "Nothing," "Rotten," and "Eh." What in the world do parents have to do to get their teens to talk to them? I asked teenagers: "What should parents do if they really want their teenager to confide in them?" They said:

▪ "Try to make them relax by holding a conversation about something else, and then start making your way through to what you think is bothering them." ERIN, 15

■ "Take a day off from work and spend it with him, and just be a friend for a change." JOHN, 18

■ "Most of the time, if parents would just listen, there would be no need to lecture. I think parents do most of the lecturing just because they're trying to keep us from making the same mistakes they made. But we might not even be thinking about making those mistakes, yet they go on and on about it." SABRINA, 14

■ "Don't jump down their throat and don't have an accusing tone. Wait until you've thought it out, and then have a rational discussion about it with them." MARITA, 16

■ "Reassure them that they won't get punished if they tell you, then keep your word." MAY, 14

■ "Go to a counseling service with your teenager, where other teenagers and parents talk about why they can't talk to each other." NICOLE, 15

■ "If you think something is on her mind, you could ask and then say, 'It's okay, you don't have to tell me now.' The majority of teenagers might say 'Wait, wait. I'll tell you.'" SHARELL, 16

■ "Hear them out without interrupting, and then reflect on your own teenage life (if you can remember), and most likely, you'll realize that not communicating is a normal problem. It's very important for teens to speak to their parents and for parents to give good advice. If he's cut off and lectured, he will seek advice from other not-so-reliable sources." SAL, 19

■ "Let him talk, and don't be angry. At least they told you." DIEDRA, 14

▩ "Stay quiet until they finish, and if you don't understand, ask, but please don't shout." VIVIAN, 16

▩ "Tell them that they can trust you, and that you won't tell anyone." NANCY, 15

▩ "Don't immediately make demands, because teenagers hate it when a parent demands something. If you talk to the teenager nicely, he will say, 'Oh, my parent cares about me.' If you scream and demand, they will say to themselves, 'The hell with you. I don't care what you say.'" ALEX, 16

Generally, teens tend to communicate with parents they can laugh and joke with, parents whose understanding they trust in. When I have asked teens why they choose one parent over another to talk to, they invariably say they choose the one who is calm, who behaves like a friend, and the one who never says things like: "That shouldn't bother you."

Nothing could be more frustrating and insulting to a teen than to hear such words, when he or she has taken the chance and confided in you. The message the teen gets is, at best, "I don't understand you," and at worst, "Something is wrong with you."

Thousands of teenagers have told me just that in their own words. And I don't think any parent would disagree with their advice. Our problem is not lack of knowledge, it's lack of self-control. But if we practice, we can change old habits. When you make a mistake, if you apologize, your teen will forgive you and give you another chance. For example, your teen confides in you, and in spite of your good intentions, you blow up or condemn him. As he's walking away saying "I knew I shouldn't have told you," do an about-face and say: "You're right, I'm sorry. I shouldn't have said that. Please continue." He may not give you an immediate chance, but soon afterward you'll get another opportunity to listen. Your teenager will give you a thousand chances, because, believe it or not, your teen needs to talk to you even more than you need to listen to your teen.

But what if, no matter what you do, your teen won't talk to you about things you feel are bothering him or her? All is not lost. Although you will lose out on knowing what's going on in your teen's mind, your teen will survive as long as he or she has another adult to confide in. Teens tell me that talking to an older brother, sister, cousin, aunt or uncle, mature friend, parents of a friend, or even a grandparent has brought them great comfort.

It's also a good idea to consider a therapist, even if your teen is not having serious problems. It's kind of an insurance policy. It can't hurt, and it very well can help. A wise, more neutral adult can be a very positive influence, and a few months of therapy now can save your teen years of therapy up the road.

A Final Note

In our great effort to get our teens to communicate with us, many of us neglect to communicate to our teens how much we appreciate, love, and admire them. A good way to do that is to write a note to your teen. A kind of sentimental one.

When my daughter was 15, I was thinking about her one evening, and in a melancholy mood, I typed her a letter and left it in her room. She didn't say anything the next day, so I asked her if she got the note. She smiled sweetly and said, "Oh yes. I did, Mommy." And that was it. Later that month I noticed the note was pasted up in her room. It remained there for at least a year. The note said:

"Dear Marthe: I was sitting in my room thinking about you. You have such a beautiful, sensitive soul that sometimes I think you should have been born with a note attached to your toes, Handle with Care. Most people can't know how intense you are, so you often get hurt. But you're a fighter. I've noticed that inner strength come through in times when you've needed it most. I know that no matter what happens to you, you're going to make it. You'll rise like a star to your destiny. I'm so happy and proud to have you as a daughter. I love you so much. Mommy"

As parents, we're often so caught up in keeping our teenagers on the right track that we neglect to stop and evaluate their good points. That is a *big* mistake. Nothing can be more encouraging and more conducive to the development of self-esteem in your teen than your taking the time to care, listen, and celebrate your teen's virtues and to express confidence that he or she will make it in life. Teens need every *crumb* of approval they can get, especially from parents. Don't feel guilty if you haven't previously done something like that for your teen. *Now is the perfect time.*

Reminders

1. When your teen is telling you about something that has happened in his or her life, don't interrupt with a reprimand or a lecture, no matter how tempted you may feel to do that. Listen, and give moral support. Then deliver your sermon a day or two later.

2. Good news: If you've alienated your teen, all is not lost. Teens are quite resilient and will give you hundreds of chances to listen and be supportive, even if they've sworn to themselves never to trust you again.

3. Teens have a whole list of things they would love to talk to their parents about, but they're afraid they will be lectured and condemned.

4. Often, when teens make provocative statements such as, "A few drinks don't affect driving ability," or "Ecstasy isn't harmful," they're really asking to be convinced to the contrary. Rather than fall into the trap of arguing, use such occasions as opportunities to calmly explain the facts.

5. When it comes to teens (and younger children, too, for that matter), honesty is the best policy. They can detect a coverup a mile away, and feel alienated and angry when we shut them out with silence or lies.

6. If your teen has trouble talking to you about sex, approach the topic from a side angle. Let your teen talk about her friends, then give your opinion about the issues.

7. Let your teen educate you. Ask him or her what is going on in the area of sex in the real world of teenagers today.

Then, in a natural way, you can exchange feelings about the issues your teen has put on the table.

8. Teens have some advice for parents. If you want your teenager to talk to you, be calm, don't condemn, act like a friend, and avoid saying things like, "That shouldn't bother you."

9. If your teen can't or won't talk to you, all is not lost. As long as your teen has another caring adult to confide in, he or she will not feel totally alienated. Sometimes a good therapist is a perfect remedy *before* your teen has serious problems.

10. Bolster your teen's self-confidence and self-esteem by taking the time to write your teen a note about his or her virtues and strengths. Whether or not he or she tells you, your teen will treasure those words, hide them in his or her heart, and remember them forever.

Chapter 9

What Teenagers Worry About

They don't have a care in the world . . . or do they? Many adults think that teenagers lead easier lives, but the truth is, they don't. They imagine that all teens are thinking about is the next party, the opposite sex, a new car, or looking better than the competition. While it is true that teenagers do enjoy devoting time and high energy to such interests (and others), they have real woes, too. Some of those woes are connected with parties, sex, cars, and the competition; but they also worry about things that perhaps you would never dream of.

What Do Teenagers Worry About?

I asked teenagers, "What are some of the typical worries that go through your mind during the course of a day?" Teens say:

■ "Whether there will be enough money for college because of my parents' tax problems and medical bills." NAOMI, 16

■ "When my parents were divorced, my mother got the short end of the deal. There's never enough money. I worry about how we're gonna live with the money we've got." JENNIFER, 16

■ "Will I be able to get all my schoolwork done? I'm under a lot of pressure right now because last year my average was low and I want to bring it up." TIM, 16

■ "I'm really scared I'll fail math and have to go to summer school." ZANE, 16

■ "My biggest worry is if I'm going to graduate next year because lately I've been messing up." MARCO, 18

■ "I'm afraid of another encounter with my father. We can't say two words to each other without a blowup. My mother always takes his side. Sometimes I think they hate me." BRUCE, 18

■ "I worry about my mother finding out my secrets." SELINA, 16

■ "I'm new in my school, and no one seems to like me. Most days it's so frustrating, I say, 'Forget about it, I'm cutting out,' but I haven't yet." XAVIER, 15

■ "I wonder why my boyfriend broke up with me. I think there must be something wrong with me since I can't keep a boyfriend." ELLEN, 15

■ "I think that people are talking about me behind my back and wonder if my so-called friends are really my friends." BOBBY, 16

■ "I worry about my weight. I'm fat, and my parents say it's only baby fat, but everyone else looks sexy, and I hate my body." ROSA, 14

■ "My complexion is gross. I have zits, and all I ever do is apply Oxy-10. I live in dread of the next pimple." TOBY, 14

■ "I think about my boyfriend. Will he find out I cheated on him?" CHANTEL, 16

■ "My mother has high blood pressure, and I never know when she'll have to go into the hospital again." RALPH, 14

■ "My mother works nights, and I always worry that

something will happen to her." ANTOINETTE, 17

▪ "My father moved out last year. I wonder what he's doing, and if he's all right." PETRA, 15

▪ "My brother plays football. I fear that he'll get badly hurt." CLEO, 15

▪ "I'm afraid my brother will turn into something bad." LEE, 14

▪ "I worry about my mother when my brother tries to use her." ANDREA, 15

▪ "My grandfather lives in Florida, and he's had two heart attacks, and God forbid, don't let him have another cause I love him a lot." ILEANA, 15

▪ "I'm afraid for my cousin. These girls are after her and they might beat her up." CORINA, 15

▪ "My mother and father are always fighting. I think they might break up." MARISOL, 15

▪ "I worry when my sister doesn't call to let us know where she is, or when my father spends the night out." VANESSA, 16

▪ "I worry that someone will come into our school and start shooting people." MADONNA, 16

▪ "I hope no one bothers me on the bus." TERRY, 17

▪ "If I die, will I go to heaven or hell?" ROCKO, 17

▪ "I worry that there will be another terrorist attack." TRISHA, 14

▪ "I think I'll pick the wrong major when I go to college— and waste a lot of time. I have no idea what I want to be yet." NICOLETTE, 17

▪ "I'm afraid there won't be any good jobs for me when I

graduate from college—who knows what the economy will be like then." GLEN, 18

▪ "I worry about my dog getting lost. Even though we keep the fence locked, sometimes he gets out, but he always comes back. What if he doesn't one day?" TOMMY, 13

▪ "I think about my grades. I wish they were higher. My sister always has higher grades than me and I can tell my parents are happy with that. I feel like I will never live up to her reputation." MYRA, 15

Teens' worries run the gamut from frivolous concerns such as physical appearance or breaking up with a boyfriend (matters that can elicit feelings of self-doubt and even lead to depression), to more obvious concerns such as school and getting along with parents, all the way up to life-and-death issues such as the health and safety in school and of family members, the date of their own death, and even the afterlife.

It's easy to make the mistake of believing that teenagers are unable to experience deep, sophisticated, intense worry, because they are often so happy-go-lucky. That joyful demeanor is not a put-on—it's the gift of youth. But at other times, teens, just like adults, entertain a host of worries, and because they don't have the experience that comes only through living, their worries often are greatly magnified; they loom large, and sometimes threaten to overwhelm them. Teenagers continually need calm reassurance from the adult world. If they get it, the worries can eventually be resolved, but if they don't, trouble lies ahead. When a teenager can't talk to either parent or another adult, and they believe no one understands how they feel, they consider suicide.

In an effort to shield their teens from adult concerns, many parents refuse to discuss things like financial problems, wayward brothers and sisters, or sick relatives. But that is a mistake. Your teenager is all too aware of such realities, but is alone in his or her worry. It's a lot better to bring things out in the open and share your problem with your teen, rather than to suffer silently with your spouse. Sharing pain with your teen will relieve him or her of the ominous feeling that something major is wrong and it's so terrible that no one will talk about it. Sharing the truth with your teen will bring you closer to each other, because you will experience each other's empathy and compassion.

What is your teenager worrying about right now? Just ask. If you phrase the question in a casual way, your teen will probably tell you. You might just say, "I'm curious. What are the typical worries that go through your mind during the course of the day?"

What Do Teenagers Think You Can Do to Help with Their Worries?

I asked teenagers, "How should parents act if they want to help teenagers to cope with their worries?" Teens have some helpful ideas:

▨ "When we talk about what's bothering us, don't just say, 'Don't worry about it.' Act as if you really understand and care." RHONDA, 14

■ "Don't act surprised and shocked when we tell you something that's bothering us. You make us feel stupid and immature." JULIESSE, 13

■ "Be calm about things. When you panic, we want to disappear from the face of the earth." LOTTY, 14

■ "They should talk to them softly, with a lot of understanding instead of screaming and yelling." MAUREEN, 15

■ "When I tell them my worry, I wish they didn't turn against me and start nagging me, making it worse. If I said I was worried about math, don't keep saying, 'I don't see you studying enough.'" DOMINIQUE, 15

■ "When we tell you, don't be so intense. Take it lightly and don't punish us if we admit doing something wrong while we're telling you what's bothering us, or we'll never trust you again." DUSTIN, 19

■ "I feel comforted when my mother brings up a verse in the Bible and tells me everything is going to work out fine." TIMMY, 19

■ "When I tell you the problem, I am asking you to keep reassuring me. I need to hear it again and again." VICTORIA, 16

■ "Give them attention in what they do (draw, write, play sports). Sit down and listen carefully. Be more of a friend than a parent." SIMON, 14

■ "Ask them if they have any problems, and talk about problems you had when you were a teenager. That makes us see your human side." GUS, 17

■ "Be honest with us." PETE, 18

When a teen has a problem, and a well-meaning parent says "Don't worry about it," a teen gets the message: You don't understand my problems. But *the teen* understands the parent is unaware of *his* or *her* reality. And the teen vows never to expose him- or herself to that parent again.

When parents act surprised that a teen has such a worry, the teen is ashamed for having the worry, and may wonder if he or she is normal. When parents become upset over the worry and overreact by shouting or punishing their teen, the teen regrets bringing it up. When parents use the expressed concern against the teen and either nag or punish (if, for example, the teen has exposed some misdeed in the course of discussing the worry), the teen will feel betrayed and will exercise great caution to keep secrets in the future.

It's not easy, but as parents we have to constantly check ourselves before we react. We have to stop, look, listen, and reflect. When a teen expresses a worry, stop yourself from talking. Then take a long, searching look at your teenager's face. If you do, you'll probably see the intensity of his or her pain. Then listen hard to what your teen's saying. Next, try to verbalize your teen's feelings in your own words. Let your teen talk. What teens really want is a listening, sympathetic ear, a little empathy and comfort, and a lot of reassurance. They long to have you talk to them as if you were more than a watchful parent. They appreciate it when you talk about your own worries and hard times as an adolescent. They don't *ever* appreciate a parent making light of their worry—so if you're tempted, don't do it.

For example, my daughter (who was much more beautiful

and shapely than I was as a teen and is much more beautiful and shapely now as an adult) once told me how upset she was because all her friends had boyfriends and she had none. She was wondering if she wasn't pretty enough. In fact, she is so pretty that people would literally stare at her in the street. I was tempted to say: "That's ridiculous. You're the prettiest girl in your school. I wish I'd looked like you when I was a teenager."

Instead, I checked myself. I thought about her problem, and then said: "When I was in high school I didn't have a boyfriend either, but for a different reason than yours. I was skinny and still nearly flat-chested, while all the other girls seemed to resemble Marilyn Monroe or Jane Russell. [I was in school during the fifties.] I think part of your problem is you're *too* attractive, and many times boys are afraid to approach a girl they think might reject them." She was amazed at what I was saying, and wanted to hear more. We talked about making guys feel at ease by giving them a simple compliment, or asking a question, or joking about something. "The idea is to break the ice by letting a guy know you are friendly and approachable," I said. She turned my advice into action, and I was soon sorry I had told her anything.

But in all seriousness, had I undermined her worry, had I said something like, "That's ridiculous, look at your shape, look how beautiful you are," I would have made her feel that something indeed must be wrong with her if, with all those assets, she still could not attract a boy. What's more, I would have been reinforcing the lie that attractiveness guarantees love from the opposite sex. We all know it takes a lot more than that, don't we!

What Do Teenagers Think Their Parents Worry About?

Teenagers in great numbers share a tendency that may surprise you: They recognize that their parents worry, but in their minds, most of their parents' worries center on one thing: the teens themselves.

▦ "When teenagers are in school, parents worry, because they cannot be with you twenty-four hours a day. They worry about what you are doing." DESIREE, 15

▦ "They worry when I'm depressed." CHRISTINE, 17

▦ "My parents worry about where I'll be in the future." THERESA, 15

▦ "My mother worries about my asthma." SISSY, 17

▦ "My mother worries about where she will get money, because my future depends on it." QUENTIN, 16

▦ "They worry about me having sex." AUDRY, 15

▦ "My parents constantly have to check that my sister and I are not using drugs. Parents don't have it easy." FRANK, 19

▦ "Your parents worry about when you go to a party, will you come home safe? They worry about who you are out with, and if you have the proper clothing and something to eat, and how we will solve our problems without them being there to help us." ORLANDO, 18

Only on rare occasions, as discussed in Chapter 4, do teenagers stop for a moment and realize that parents are not just parents, but full-fledged people with a whole lot of additional concerns that may have nothing to do with their teenagers. Their view is still largely egocentric, and quite normal for teenagers. They are, after all, still part child.

But the teens do have a point. While our worries are not 100 percent related to them, they are probably at least 75 percent related. And much of our concern is the world they're growing up in. Drugs, sexual promiscuity and diseases, safety in school, weapons, shootings and other violence, terrorist threats, the threat of nuclear war, and changing technology are all threats to us as parents. We feel sorry for our teens and often wish we could turn back the clock for them. But do teens share this view? Do they fear the world they're living in and wish they were living in the fifties or sixties?

How Do Teens Feel about the World They're Living In?

I asked teenagers: "Parents say, 'I feel sorry for teenagers growing up today. There are so many more temptations and threats than there were in our day: drugs, sexual promiscuity and diseases, violence, terrorists, and the threat of a nuclear war.' How do you feel about your world as compared to how it was when your parents were teenagers?" Their answers are uplifting:

■ "Today almost everybody goes to college—even minorities. In my mother's day it wasn't quite that way." GERARD, 16

■ "Back then AIDS was a new thing. Now we know more about it and can take precautions." CAMMY, 15

▓ "My father had four brothers and sisters, and lived in the projects. He was poor. We own a house in the middle-class neighborhood, and I lack nothing. How could I complain?" MEGAN, 16

▓ "I can e-mail my friends back and forth on the Internet and even have a conversation with ten friends at a time in a chat room. My mother had to rely on the phone!" TAMMY, 16

▓ "Today women can become congresswomen and who knows, even president. In my mother's day women were not thinking of that yet." DONNA, 15

▓ "We have better technology: computers, CDs, DVDs, cell phones, MP3s. My mother said when she was a teen nobody had notebook computers because they were too expensive, and nobody had cell phones. Nobody." EDMUND, 15

It's easy to feel sorry for teenagers if we forget that in many ways they do feel comfortable in the world they live in because they were born into it. They wouldn't turn the clock back for anything. It's the parents who sometimes want to do that, because we miss the good old days when things were more simple and safe. Some of us are not happy about advancing technology.

Please don't misunderstand. I'm not diminishing the very real dangers in what seems to me to be an increasingly corrupt world, and the constant need to be vigilant as our teens explore it. Let's take the Internet for example: We need to block porno and other offensive sites available to our teens, and keep both eyes glued to the screen—during and after our teens sign on-line—even if it does make us feel a little guilty for spying.

Better to be overly cautious than to find out our teens have gotten caught up in something damaging on the Internet. Thankfully there are safety precautions parents can put in place to prevent teens from going to certain sites. But we can't be everywhere. That's where communicating one-on-one with our teens comes in.

What's most important, however, is the attitude of our teenagers. It's positive. We can call it the optimism of youth, if we wish, but whatever we do, let's keep encouraging our teens to face the challenges ahead of them with the sense of excitement they now possess, and continue to instill values that will surface later and help them to make wise decisions as life's problems arise.

Reminders

1. Teenagers worry about things that may surprise their parents. Inquire, and you will learn what some of those things are.
2. Teens appreciate it when parents bring things out in the open and discuss family worries with them.
3. When teens are worried, the last thing they want to hear from a parent is, "Don't worry about it."
4. Teens like to hear about things that parents worried about when they were teenagers. It makes them feel confident that they, too, will survive those and other potential disasters.
5. Teens believe that most of their parents' worries revolve around them. Are they right?

6. Teens are not as worried as their parents are about the world they live in. Teens are excited about the future and are glad they are teenagers today rather than in an earlier decade. It's the parents who want to turn back the clock.

7. When teens are worried, they look for a listening ear, but most of all, they want reassurance.

Chapter 10
Keep On Keeping On

■ ■ ■

Parents work hard warning their teens about potential danger, in the hope that their words are not going in one ear, and out the other. Even though half the time your teenager may look distracted while you're talking, or says, "I know, I know," and looks bored, your teen's probably absorbing a lot more than you think. Here's proof.

Your Warnings and Lectures Are Not in Vain

I asked teenagers if they were ever about to do something wrong, and their parents' words came back to haunt them. I asked if they did the deed anyway, or if they stopped themselves. Here's what they said:

■ "My mother is always preaching about the way smoking pot destroys brain cells. So one day I was with my friend and he was smoking a joint, and he offered me one. My mother's words came to mind and I said, 'No, that's all right. I'm not into that, but it's okay if you do it.' In the meantime I was thinking 'He's rotting out his brain.'" GEORGE, 13

■ "I went to a party with my friends and it was nice, and everyone was having a good time. Later on my friend started doing lines of coke. There were ten of us. I was the only one not doing coke. They started to get upset, so I was about to do a line to prove that I wasn't scared. Then I remembered things my mother said: 'Who cares what everyone else says? They can call you names, but words don't hurt. They're only ruining themselves.' So I turned them down. They were mad, but I felt good about myself." JOHN, 17

"Sometimes when my friends want me to hang out with them, and I'm depressed and tempted to go with them even though I know I have schoolwork to do, my mother's words come to mind: 'If you put in the minimum effort, don't expect to go to Harvard.' Then I think of my future and I put my studies first." JANE, 14

"One day some of my friends wanted to cut school and go to the park, but my mother's words haunted me: 'You can fool everyone else, but you can't fool yourself.' I didn't cut, because I thought that even if I get away with it, it was me who would miss important work that might be on the test, and I would only be fooling myself." ROCHELLE, 16

"I was about to have sex with this guy, but something stopped me. I was hanging out with this group of friends, and we decided to go to my friend's house. We all went down to the basement, put on the radio, and we just started talking. All of a sudden the lights went out, and I knew from that point something was up. I really liked the guy a lot. I had been going with him for a year. I thought to myself 'If I don't do it with him, he'll probably break up with me,' and that was the last thing I wanted to happen. So I finally decided I would go all the way with him. But as soon as he went for my pants, I pushed him away. For some reason I heard my mother's voice saying: 'Think of the big picture. One mistake can ruin your life.' As soon as I heard that, I jumped off the couch and told my boyfriend I just wasn't ready, and that if he can't handle that, just get the hell out of my life. Sex isn't everything." CAPRI, 15

■ "My boyfriend asked me to have sex with him. I didn't know what to say. I was about to say yes, but I was scared because I had never done this before. Then I heard my mother's voice say: 'Boys will say anything to get what they want. If you do what they say, you'll be sorry the next day. But if you don't you'll never be sorry. Don't do something you will regret.' I kept hearing that voice saying, 'Don't do something you will regret,' over and over again, and I couldn't go through with it." NANETTE, 16

■ "One day my friends asked me to go with them in this car that they had stolen. They said, 'Oh, come on, don't act like an old man before your time.' I was bored and looking for some fun, but my mother's words came to me: 'Don't follow the crowd, because it will lead you to the worst.' I didn't go, and I was lucky, because they got picked up by the police." ERROL, 16

■ "I had a terrible fight with my parents, and I was so depressed, I thought that I wasn't worth anything because they usually picked on me, and I thought why should I live? So I took a bottle of pills my mother had in the medicine cabinet and a glass of water. But when I was about to put the pills in my mouth, I heard my mother's voice saying: 'God sent you to this world for a purpose. Nobody knows what that purpose is now, but if you get through the bad times, you'll find out.' That's when I realized what I was doing. I closed the bottle and wiped the tears and got on my knees and started praying for

Keep On Keeping On

God's forgiveness. If it wasn't for that little voice, God knows where I would be now." MIRIAM, 16

■ "I was out with a bunch of friends and it was about 2 A.M., and we were coming home from a party. There were no cops around, so they all decided to jump the turnstile. They did it, and I was about to, when I heard my mother's voice: 'If I ever get a call from the police, you'll spend the night in jail. Then after I come and get you, I'll beat you half to death.' As you can guess, I paid my fare." MONIQUE, 17

■ "When my grandmother gets on my nerves, and I'm ready to be disrespectful to her, I hear my mother's words: 'If it wasn't for your grandma, you wouldn't be here.' I walk away and keep my mouth shut because I know it's the truth." CHRIS, 17

■ "I was going to sell drugs, but my mother's words came to me loud and clear: 'What's done in the darkness shall come to light.' I thought, 'Hey, I have my whole life in front of me. Why spend it in jail?'" TYRONE, 17

■ "My mother always says: 'Think before you act.' In many cases it stopped me from making the wrong move, because I hesitated and thought things through." JACK, 19

Too good to be true? Of course it is if we're foolish enough to think that every single time our teenager is about to do something wrong, he or she immediately hears our voice and, like a robot, stops. But the fact is, many times our lectures, our warnings, and our words of encouragement come to our teens' minds just when they're needed most.

Teens Say, Keep On Keeping On

Do teenagers want you to keep lecturing, even though they complain bitterly about your nagging? I asked teenagers: "Do you think parents should keep on giving lectures as to what is right and wrong, even if you appear not to listen?" Teens say:

▦ "Yes. Because someday it will click, and the light will come, and even if you didn't follow it in your teenage stages, you'll do the right thing, and then you'll be just like your parents to your kids." NATASHA, 15

▦ "Yes, because even though we appear not to listen, we still do, and believe me, it stays with us." FREDDY, 18

▦ "I think they should. Kids tend to look not interested because they want their parents to stop talking, but if you do stop talking, your kids will think they won and you'll never have control of them. If you keep on talking, even if they don't seem interested, they may be listening and may even understand what you're saying." JENNIFER, 16

▦ "Yes, because they are always right in the end." GLORIA, 17

▦ "Yes. It will sink through our thick heads one of these days, after she said it a million times." DESI, 15

▦ "Yes. It sometimes saves your life." KENNY, 14

▦ "Yes. It shows they care. Later you will know what to do in a situation." SHARI, 13

▦ "Yes, and always stick to your guns, even though your teenagers seem not to be listening. Never change your opinion." DAVE, 19

■ "Yes, because if you don't, they will never get it through their heads." BRIAN, 15

I wish my own father were still alive so I could tell him how the words he spoke to me served to become the driving force of my life. At the time I brushed them away and acted as if I wasn't really interested in hearing them. He knew that I was discouraged to see my sister get higher marks even though she put in much less effort than I did. Seeing my frustration, he would take me aside and give me this little lecture: "Joyce," he would say, "remember the story of the tortoise and the hare. Because the hare was quick, he knew he didn't have to work as hard, so he went to sleep and, in the end, lost the race. But the tortoise, who no one believed in, knew he had to keep going in order to win, so he kept on moving. He knew that no one expected him to succeed, and this inspired him to try even harder. He won the race because he knew that it isn't just talent that brings success, but also persistence and continual effort. If you learn this lesson early in life, with your intelligence and creativity, it's inevitable that you'll succeed."

I can honestly say I don't know if, without those words, I would have kept on plodding through all the years when my hard work seemed to be in vain—when I got myriad rejection slips for my first book, *I Dare You;* when, so many times, I was tempted to give up when the going got rough as I worked my way toward my Ph.D. in English Literature at NYU. Remembering his words, I kept telling myself, "I'll keep going. If I don't make it, at least I'll be able to say it wasn't because I gave up. It will be because I simply couldn't do it." I got my

Ph.D., and *I Dare You* was published not only in hardcover but in paperback, too. I have had many books published and needless to say, there's a thread running through them, a theme that sounds a lot like my father's message to me. Think of your own life. Which of your parents' warnings and lectures serve to this day to make you a stronger, happier, better person?

It may not always seem as though you're getting through to your teenager, but just imagine what would happen if you didn't give any lectures or speeches. Imagine what might (or might not) transpire if your son or daughter had nothing from you to refer to—no tape recording of mommy's or daddy's voice to measure him- or herself against. So no matter how unlikely it seems that you're getting through, keep on keeping on. Remember, it's not the short run that counts (the moments when they rebel and turn away), but the long run—the time when they will piece together all that they have learned and make a success of their lives.

And finally, give yourself a break. You're only human. If you were the perfect parent (if there is such a thing), your offspring would still have a will of their own. They're not clones. They make conscious decisions for themselves, and there are other forces influencing them—your spouse, the media, friends and relations, teachers, the books they read, and so on. You can't take all the blame if things don't turn out exactly as you had dreamed, just as you can't take all the credit if they exceed your highest expectations. All you can do is your best. The rest is up to your teen.

Reminders

1. Good news. Teenagers admit that at crucial moments, parents' words come to their minds to keep them from doing something wrong or inspire them to do the right thing.

2. Although teens often appear not to be listening, they admit that they are. They say they want parents to continue to lecture them on what is right and wrong, and believe that in the end, it's your teachings that will keep them on the right track.

3. Think of your own life. What effect did your parents' warnings and inspirational sermons have upon your life?

4. If you gave up and stopped talking, imagine what would happen! Your teen would have no voice in the back of his or her mind to measure him- or herself against.

5. You're so busy trying to cope with your teenager, it's easy to be discouraged and think that all of your hard work is in vain. It isn't. You'll see the results later. Years later. In the meantime, keep on keeping on. Remember, not *everything* is your fault. Do your best. After that, it's in God's hands.

Appendix

Questions
for Teenagers

Parents, here's a way to get to know your teen better. Copy this section and ask your teen to fill it out. Then you can have an interesting discussion after you read his or her answers. If your teen won't do it for you, give the questions to a friend who knows your teen, and have the friend ask your teen to fill it out. (This often works better.) Once you see the answers, you can have some lively discussions with your teen about the topics covered in the questionnaire. Good luck.

1. What do your parents complain about when they spend money on you?

2. What do you expect your parents to buy you that they don't really want to buy you?

3. What makes you think they *should* buy it for you?

4. How would you feel if you learned your parents had to give up something they really wanted in order to buy something *you* really wanted?

5. When your parents give you money for things that you want, do you appreciate it? Why do you sometimes neglect to thank them or to show appreciation?

6. What is the most generous thing your parents ever did for you? How did you feel when they did it? Did you tell them how you felt, or did you keep it to yourself? Why?

7. What have your parents done for you lately?

8. What do you do that your parents claim is irresponsible?

9. What goes through your mind when you're about to be irresponsible and you know it? Give a specific example.

10. Give an example of when you failed to meet a deadline in a school situation. Tell exactly what went through your mind when you thought about the deadline and decided not to meet it.

11. When do your parents call you lazy? Are you lazy? Why? What don't your parents understand?

12. When did you last fail to do a chore you were supposed to do? Why didn't you do it? What did you say to yourself when you thought of doing it?

13. Name some things you do that your parents are always calling a waste of time. Are they right? Why do you do those things?

14. What don't your parents understand about the things you do that they say are a waste of time?

15. What activities do your parents tell you to engage in more often? List them. Then tell why you don't want to spend more time on those activities.

16. Does your father or mother ever wear something that you think looks ridiculous (for example, out of style, too young for his or her age, inappropriate)? Give an example.

17. Why do you think it's necessary for you to correct your parents when they wear something that you think looks ridiculous?

18. Did you ever tell your divorced or separated parent that you didn't like someone he or she was dating? Why?

19. Describe a time when you thought your parent was behaving in an immature or embarrassing manner. What went through your mind at the time?

20. Did you ever defy your parents and do exactly what they forbade you to do? Why did you do it?

21. Did you ever feel sorry for your mother or father? Give an example.

22. Give an example of a friend, acquaintance, boyfriend, or girlfriend that your parents didn't approve of. Why didn't they approve?

23. Did you ever end up rejecting a friend, acquaintance, boyfriend, or girlfriend because you realized that your parents were right? Explain the situation.

24. Did you ever tell your parents that they were right about that person? Why or why not?

25. If you were the parent of a teenager, what sort of friend would you not want your teen to hang out with and why?

26. What advice do you have for parents who disapprove of their teenagers' friends?

27. What is the most embarrassing thing your parent ever said or did to one of your friends? What went through your mind when your parent did this?

28. Name three things you do that drive your mother or father up the wall. If you know it drives them crazy, why do you do it anyway?

29. Think of one thing that your mother or father does that annoys you. Would you be willing to make a trade with your parents? You stop doing one specific thing that drives them up the wall in exchange for their giving up

something that drives you up the wall? What specific trade would you make?

30. Why do you come home late for dinner, even though you know it causes your parents great inconvenience?

31. For girls, why do you borrow your mother's makeup, shampoo, or clothing, without asking, even though you know it bothers her?

32. At what age do you think parents should stop telling their children how to dress? Why?

33. If you were a parent of a teen, would you put any restriction at all on the way your teen dressed? What rules would you make and why?

34. What is the most outrageous outfit you ever wore, and what did your parents say about it?

35. When did your parent ever criticize your hairstyle? What did he or she say? What went through your mind when your parent said that?

36. Looking back on your life, can you now see that the way you dressed or wore your hair at a certain time was ridiculous and that you would never dress or wear your hair that way now? When did you look like that and what sort of look did it give you? Why wouldn't you want to look that way now?

37. If you could teach parents a lesson about the way teenagers dress and wear their hair, what lesson would that be?

38. What specific subject could you never talk to your parents about and why?

39. Did you ever try to talk to your mother or father about the way you really feel about sex? What happened?

40. If you didn't try to talk to your parents about a difficult subject, why didn't you?

41. Think of a time when you started telling your mother or father something that happened to you, and before you got the story out, they started giving you a lecture. Did you finish telling the story? Why or why not? How did that make you feel?

42. What advice would you give parents for when their teenagers start telling them something and they may feel the impulse to interrupt or dismiss the discussion?

43. If you can't talk to either parent, why not? Whom do you confide in? Do you sometimes wish you could express yourself more freely to your parents? Why?

44. What are some of the typical worries that go through your mind during the day?

45. What is worrying you the most right at this moment? Why?

46. What was your greatest worry one year ago, and how do you feel about that problem now?

47. What do your parents worry about? In your opinion,

whose worries do you believe are more serious: yours or your parents? Why?

48. People say it's hard growing up in the new millennium. Do you feel you'd have been more at ease as a teenager in an earlier decade, or are you glad you're a teenager now? Why?

49. Give an example of a time when you were about to do something wrong, and something your mother or father said came to your mind. Did you do it anyway or did you stop yourself? Explain the situation.

50. Do you think parents should keep on giving lectures as to what is right and what is wrong, even if their kids appear not to listen? Why?

Bibliography of Joyce Vedral Books and Tapes

■ ■ ■

Fitness Books

Vedral, Joyce, Ph.D. *Toning for Teens.* New York: Warner Books, 2002.

———. *The Bathing Suit Workout.* New York: Warner Books, 1999.

———. *Bone Building Body Shaping Workout.* New York: Simon & Schuster, 1998.

———. *Weight Training Made Easy: From Beginner to Expert in Four Simple Steps.* New York: Warner Books, 1997.

———. *Definition: Shape Without Bulk in Fifteen Minutes a Day.* New York: Warner Books, 1995.

———. *Top Shape.* New York: Warner Books, 1995.

———. *Bottoms Up!* New York: Warner Books, 1993.

———. *Gut Busters.* New York: Warner Books, 1992.

———. *The Fat-Burning Workout.* New York: Warner Books, 1991.

———. *The 12-Minute Total-Body Workout.* New York: Warner Books, 1989.

———. *Now or Never.* New York: Warner Books, 1986.

Self-Help Book

Vedral, Joyce, Ph.D. *Get Rid of Him.* New York: Warner Books, 1993.

Self-Help Audiotape

This tape is found only at *www.joycevedral.com.*

Vedral, Joyce, Ph.D. *Look In, Look Up—Look Out!! Be the Person You Were Meant to Be.* New York: Warner Books, 1996.

Exercise Videos and DVDs

These are found only at *www.joycevedral.com* or
1-877-JVEDRAL (1-877-583-3725).

Vedral, Joyce, Ph.D. *Bone Building Body Shaping Workout.* Joycercize Inc., 2003.

————. *Bottoms Up Gold Plus Upper, Lower and Middle Body Workout.* Joycercize Inc., 2003.

————. *Joyce Vedral's Interval Aerobics.* Joycercize Inc., 2003.

————. *Joyce Vedral's Easy Does It: The Totally Relaxing Total Body Stretch System.* Joycercize Inc., 2003.

————. *Gut, Love Handle, Pooch Busters.* Joycercize Inc., 2001.

————. *Joyce Explains.* Joycercize Inc., 2001.

————. *Non-Stop.* Joycercize Inc., 2001.

————. *Reshape Your Body in 12 Minutes a Day: Dynamic Tension.* Joycercize Inc., 2001.

————. *Workout 101.* Joycercize Inc., 2001.

————. *The Bathing Suit Workout.* Joycercize Inc., 2000.

————. *Fast Forward: Reshape Your Body after Weight Gain, Pregnancy, Sticking Points and Neglect.* Joycercize Inc., 2000.

————. *The Fat Burning Workout.* Joycercize Inc., 2000.

————. *Weight Training Made Easier.* Joycercize Inc., 2000.

————. *The Definition Workout: Upper, Lower and Middle Body,* Joycercize Inc., 1999.

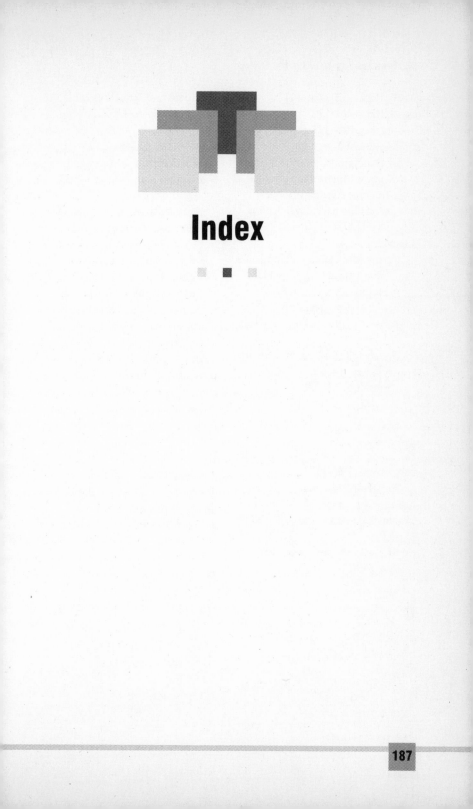

Index

F

fighting, 60–62, 70
friends
    behavior in front of, 78–86, 91
    criticism of, 72–73, 82
    flirting with, 86
    influence of, 88–91
    parental influence on selection
      of, 74–77, 90
    teen evaluations of, 77–78
future, discussing teens', 138

G

girlfriends, 58–59, 86–88, 91,
    139–140
gum, cracking, 100–101

H

hair, 118–119
    absorbing parents' standards
      for, 122
    criticism of mothers', 51–52, 69
    See also appearance
homework, 31–33, 45
honesty, importance of, 140, 149
honor, sense of, 60

I

individuality, encouraging, 68–79
information, getting about teens'
    lives, 82–83
insensitivity, 36
Internet, 162–163

K, L

knowledge, 66–68, 70
language, 101–104, 112
lateness, 33–36, 45
lectures, effectiveness of, 166–173
life experience, 66–70
listening, 141, 150
    and teen worries, 158–159

M

makeup
    criticism of mothers', 51–52, 69
    forbidding, 117
      See also appearance
money, 10–14
morals, 135
mothers, criticism of hair and
    makeup of, 51–52, 69
motivation
    for doing chores, 28–30
    for responsible behavior, 36–39
    for schoolwork, 32–33
    suggestions regarding, 45
music, 95–96, 111

N

nagging, 109
neglecting, 22–23

P

physical violence, 84–85
pregnancy, 143
procrastination, 27–28, 44–45

About the Author

Joyce Vedral earned a Ph.D. in English literature with a specialization in psychology from New York University. She is a former English teacher who taught teenagers at the high school level for twenty years and also taught at Pace University in New York City.

While teaching high schools students, she shortly became known as a miracle-worker, the one teacher who would take in those "impossible" kids. After being shunted from one class to another, these troubled teens would often make a positive change after working with Joyce. Equally as popular with the parents as with the students, it was not unusual to overhear an irate parent ask for Joyce, claiming "She's the only one I'll talk to!"

Joyce has had plenty of first-hand parenting experience through her daughter and her many nieces and nephews. But there's more to Joyce than you may realize. She is a *New York Times*, *USA Today*, and *Publishers Weekly* bestselling author whose fitness books and videos have sold more than three million copies. She has been on the *New York Times* and *USA Today* bestseller lists four times and is the author of the #1 *New York Times* bestseller *Bottoms Up!*, as well as her recently published and pediatrician-recommended book, *Toning for Teens*. Joyce also has one of the most popular Web sites on the Internet where she gives free fitness advice.

Joyce has appeared frequently on *Oprah*, *Montel Williams*, *Jenny Jones*, CNN, *The Today Show*, and others. She has been quoted by numerous newspapers and appeared on countless radio shows. In addition, Joyce is an in-demand lecturer. In the words of Paul Adamo, formerly of the Learning Annex, "In all the years of my having lectures, I've never seen an audience react to anyone the way they react to Joyce. People walk away with love in their hearts. A relationship develops. It's something to see."

Please visit her Web site at *www.joycevedral.com*.